POSTCARD HISTORY SERIES

Chicago Skyscrapers
in Vintage Postcards

MONTGOMERY WARD & CO. BUILDING. In the early 1900s, many visitors to Chicago took in the view from the observation deck of the Montgomery Ward & Co. Building. Afterwards, they often sent home souvenir postcards with poems like the one inscribed here. (1905)

POSTCARD HISTORY SERIES

Chicago Skyscrapers

IN VINTAGE POSTCARDS

Leslie A. Hudson

ARCADIA
PUBLISHING

Published by Arcadia Publishing
Charleston SC, Chicago IL, Portsmouth NH, San Francisco CA

Printed in the United States of America

Library of Congress Catalog Card Number: 2004110522

For all general information contact Arcadia Publishing at:
Telephone 843-853-2070
Fax 843-853-0044
E-mail sales@arcadiapublishing.com
For customer service and orders:
Toll-Free 1-888-313-2665

Visit us on the Internet at www.arcadiapublishing.com

(Front cover)
SKYLINE FROM LAKE MICHIGAN AT THE MOUTH OF THE CHICAGO RIVER, C. 1933. These skyscrapers were all constructed within a ten-year period, and all but two are located on North Michigan Avenue. The Wrigley Building is the earliest of the group, begun in 1919, and the Carbide and Carbon Building and Medinah Athletic Club were constructed last, in 1929. (MRS)

(Back cover)
VIEW SOUTH ALONG MICHIGAN AVENUE, FROM THE ART INSTITUTE. Across the street, from right to left, are the Railway Exchange Building, the Stratford Hotel, and the McCormick Building. The rooftops of the Illinois Central Depot can be seen in the distance, just to the right of the flagpole. (DP)

MICHIGAN AVENUE, LOOKING NORTH FROM THE BLACKSTONE HOTEL TO THE DRAKE, C. 1920. Many recognizable buildings along the length of Michigan Avenue, from Grant Park to the Oak Street Beach, as well as some in the Loop, to the left, appear in this view. (MRS)

CONTENTS

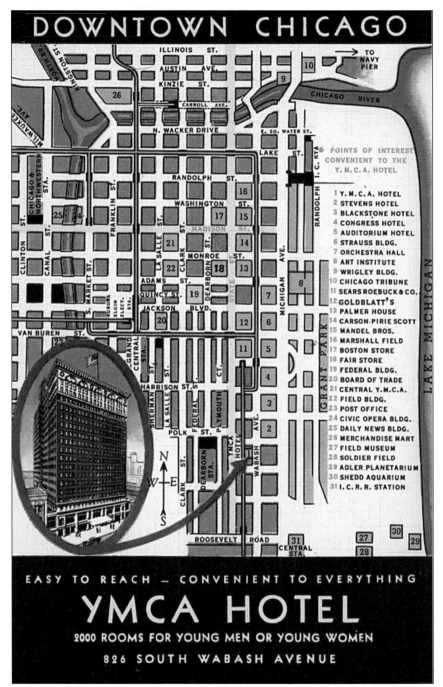

YMCA Hotel with Chicago Loop Map. The YMCA Hotel, designed by Robert C. Berlin and built in 1916, was converted into apartments in 1988 and today is known as the Burnham Park Plaza. The map on this postcard depicts Chicago's "Loop" district, where most of the buildings in this book are, or were, located. (CT-**1943**)

INTRODUCTION

In 1884, for a site on La Salle Street in downtown Chicago, an architect and engineer by the name of William Le Baron Jenney designed a nine-story office building that used iron and steel in its construction. Supported by an internal metal frame rather than its walls, this building, the Home Insurance Building, is generally considered the first skyscraper ever constructed.

What is a skyscraper and why did it develop in Chicago? A skyscraper is, quite simply, a very tall building. The term "skyscraper" was first used in 1888 in a description of Chicago's tall structures, but more often these early buildings were just called "high buildings" or "tall buildings." Several important technological and social developments coincided in Chicago to make the skyscraper possible and practical. Metal framing techniques like those developed by Jenney in the Home Insurance Building made it possible to erect buildings taller than masonry walls had allowed. The invention of safer, high-speed elevators made it practical to create office space many stories above the ground. Techniques for foundation construction, especially important in Chicago with its soft clay soil and bedrock 125 feet below grade, were devised to support the weight of larger buildings. The invention of the Bessemer steel process and lightweight steel-frame construction made it possible to rapidly erect ever-higher buildings.

Design developments occurred in tandem with the technological. Once walls no longer needed to provide support, window openings could be enlarged. Eventually entire exteriors were sheathed in glass and terra-cotta, as seen on the Reliance Building (1895). This type of exterior, "hung" on the structural frame, is called a "curtain wall." The "Chicago window"—a three-part window with a wide fixed pane and narrow movable sash windows on either side—developed at this time. Often the underlying steel frame was revealed by the arrangement of spandrels (space between the window sills and top of windows below) and piers (vertical structural supports) on the façade; this is also characteristic of buildings designed during this period.

Following the Chicago Fire of 1871 the city rebuilt itself and grew at a phenomenal rate. The pressure of land values in downtown Chicago in the 1880s and demand for modern office space encouraged property owners to maximize the use of the property by building multi-storied structures. Hired by businessmen to design buildings for purely commercial purposes, a group of young Chicago architects that included Jenney, Daniel Burnham, John Root, and Louis Sullivan designed many tall commercial buildings in the 1880s and 1890s. This came to be known as the Chicago School of architecture.

The public's reaction to these new structures was usually amazement. The Manhattan Building (1891) was called "Hercules" by visitors to the 1893 World's Columbian Exposition. The Montgomery Wards & Company Building (1899), Masonic Temple (1891-92), Auditorium Building (1887-89), and Majestic Building (1905) all had observation towers that allowed visitors to enjoy spectacular views from the sky. The buildings also provoked a range of negative reactions. There was a prejudice that buildings designed for such commercial purposes could not have artistic value. Some critics called the buildings "monstrosities" that "disfigured" the city. There was concern about the possible "collapsing of one of these monster structures on a crowded street." Complaints that the tall buildings blocked the sky and darkened the streets persisted, with some justification, and led to city zoning ordinances that limited building height. A zoning law passed in 1923 required setbacks above the 22nd floor (and inadvertently helped to create the distinctive Art Deco skyscraper forms built during the next decade).

In the 1890s and early 1900s, Chicago's visitors and residents did what people throughout the country were doing—they sent and collected postcards. This postcard craze, beginning with the introduction of picture postcards at Chicago's 1893 World's Columbian Exposition, has left us with a wealth of images and messages that provide clues to the public's reaction to the city and its architecture.

> *I tried to see you from the top, nothing doing. —1906.*
> Montgomery Ward & Co. Tower.

> *This is a beautiful bldg. inside. Has paintings on the walls & marble floors. Just an office bldg too. —1905.*
> Marquette Building.

Chicago, the birthplace of the skyscraper, has never stopped building. The city's skyline and streetscape remain in a perpetual state of change. Although Chicago has changed greatly since William Le Baron Jenney's Home Insurance Building was erected in 1885, with these postcards we are able to glimpse views of a Chicago long gone, when the ideas of skyscrapers were first being explored.

ABOUT THIS BOOK

Most of the buildings discussed in this book are skyscrapers, but the occasional non-skyscraper has been included when it is of historical or architectural interest. The time period covered is 1866 to 1935 (construction dates of buildings depicted); the postcards themselves date from 1900 to 1950. Buildings have been arranged geographically (by street), rather than chronologically, to facilitate walking to the buildings and sites of former buildings. Each chapter includes a map. In the captions, I use the following convention for the main listing of each building:

Building Name [Building Status **(D or E)**]. Name of architect(s), date constructed; building address (Map location, e.g., **M2**).

Building Status code:
D=Demolished
E=Extant

Map code:
M=Michigan Avenue (at Grant Park)
W=Wabash Avenue
S=State Street
D=Dearborn Street
C=Clark Street
L=La Salle Street
R=Along the River and North Michigan Avenue

Occasionally I've included something to look for if you visit the building. These suggestions are indicated as follows: (v). Publication information and dates for the postcards are provided, when known, at the end of each caption. For an explanation of this, please see "Image Sources" on page 126.

One

MICHIGAN AVENUE

Michigan Avenue was originally called Michigan Boulevard (or "Boul Mich") and initially extended only southward from the Chicago River. Along Grant Park it developed as a one-sided street, with structures erected on the west side to face Lake Michigan and what was then called Lake Front Park. Following the Great Fire of 1871, Michigan Avenue was redeveloped into a fashionable street lined with hotels, residences, and buildings that housed the city's cultural institutions. The residences gradually gave way to larger structures but appear in a few of the early postcards included here. Because of their high visibility and premium siting, buildings along Michigan Avenue were among the most expensive and, as these postcards show, the most highly-detailed in the city. Laws enacted to prohibit construction on the east side of Michigan Avenue and the creation of Grant Park have maintained the one-sided character of these blocks that came to be called the "Michigan Avenue Cliff" or "Michigan Avenue Streetwall." In 2002, the stretch of Michigan Avenue between 11th Street and Randolph Street was designated the "Historic Michigan Boulevard District," a Chicago Landmark.

MICHIGAN BOULEVARD AT NIGHT. ". . . [T]ake your stand on Michigan Ave. between the hours of seven and eight on almost any evening of the week. The attractive shop windows are alive with light and color, while away down at Twelfth St. . . . twinkle and flash the myriad lights of gorgeous electric signs, the city even in play time not quite forgetting business. Equally fascinating to the onlooker are the thousands of blazing, bobbing headlights of automobiles that whir swiftly up and down the broad avenue. All Chicago seems out 'joy riding' or headed for the theaters. . . ." (*Rand McNally's Souvenir Guide to Chicago*, 1912). (VOH-**1911**)

Michigan Avenue
(at Grant Park)

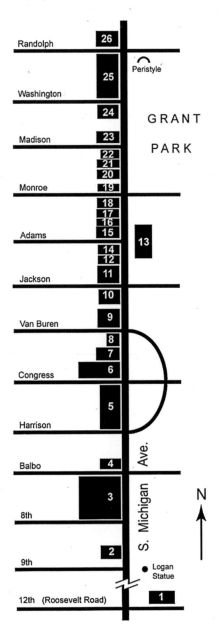

M1. Illinois Central Depot
M2. YWCA Hotel
M3. Stevens Hotel
   (Chicago Hilton & Towers)
M4. Blackstone Hotel
M5. Auditorium Annex/Congress Hotel
M6. Auditorium Building
M7. Studebaker Building
   (Fine Arts Building)
M8. Chicago Club
M9. McCormick Building
M10. Stratford Hotel; Straus Building
   (Britannica Center)
M11. Railway Exchange Building
   (Santa Fe Center)
M12. Thomas Orchestra Hall
M13. Art Institute of Chicago
M14. Pullman Building
M15. Peoples Gas Building
M16. Lake View Building
M17. Illinois Athletic Club
M18. Monroe Building
M19. University Club
M20. Millinery Building
M21. Chicago Athletic Association
M22. Willoughby Tower
M23. Montgomery Ward & Co. Tower Building
M24. Michigan Boulevard Building
M25. Chicago Public Library
   (Chicago Cultural Center)
M26. John Crerar Library

GRANT PARK AND ILLINOIS CENTRAL DEPOT, CHICAGO, ILL.

Copyright 1906, by The Cas R. rence Co., Chicago.

GRANT PARK AND ILLINOIS CENTRAL DEPOT. This scene looks south on Michigan Avenue towards 12th Street and the Illinois Central Depot. A row of Italianate-style residences called "Park Row" appears to the right of the depot (see also next). These fashionable homes faced Grant Park, then just a narrow strip between Michigan Avenue and the railroad tracks. (v The statue on the knoll, opposite 9th Street, remains. It was erected in 1897 to honor the Civil War general and Memorial Day founder, John A. Logan.) (VOH-**1906**)

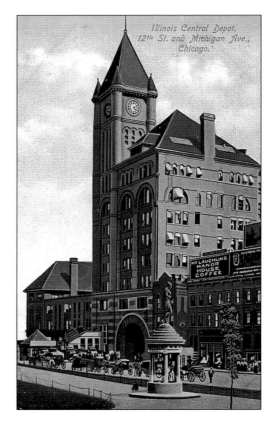

Illinois Central Depot, 12th St. and Michigan Ave., Chicago.

ILLINOIS CENTRAL DEPOT [D]. Bradford L. Gilbert, 1892; 12th Street and Michigan Avenue (**M1**). The Illinois Central Depot stood at the south end of Grant Park for more than 80 years and served the New York Central Railroad, Illinois Central Railroad, and commuter trains. Built for the World's Columbian Exposition, in the 20th century the depot was the Chicago entry point for many African Americans migrating north. In 1974, after Amtrak consolidated intercity service at Union Station, the station was demolished and the site absorbed by Grant Park. (1909)

YOUNG WOMEN'S CHRISTIAN ASSOCIATION HOTEL [E]. John M. Van Osdel II, 1894; 830 S. Michigan Avenue (**M2**). In 1909, a Chicago visitor sent the following postcard message: "Dear Mother. We reached Chicago today about 20 minutes late. Very hot here. I went to the Y.W.C.A. Handy to the station. Got a good bath and rested, also my meals. Am well. Will write more later—with love, M." (v This lovely building has remained surprisingly unchanged. Although the bricks have been painted blue and at present the building is empty and needs restoration, the cornice, columns, and other terra-cotta ornamentation remain. Even the outline of the lettering, "The Young Women's Christian Asso," can still be seen above the doorway. Because the property is included in the recently-designated Historic Michigan Boulevard District, it will be protected and, one hopes, restored.) (CT-1909)

AEROPLANE VIEW OF THE 830 SOUTH MICHIGAN HOTEL. In later years the YWCA Hotel became the "830 South Michigan Hotel." The caption on reverse reads: "On the famous Michigan Blvd. in the best Hotel, Theater, and Shopping District. Within a few minutes walk from Illinois Central, Grand Central Stations and the 'Loop.' Ample Parking Space adjoining Hotel. Excellent food in our Dining Room at moderate prices. Only 1/2 block South of the Stevens Hotel, yet at half its rates." (CT)

THE STEVENS HOTEL [E]. Holabird & Roche, 1922–1927; 720 S. Michigan Avenue (**M3**). The Stevens Hotel, designed to be the "largest and most sumptuous hotel" in the world, originally contained 3,000 guestrooms and a convention hall that seated 4,000. A rooftop golf course was called the "Hi Ho Golf Club." The tiny YWCA Hotel appears in this view, third building from the left. (v A small museum off the lobby explains the history of the Stevens Hotel.) (1938)

THE STEVENS HOTEL, AS ARMY AIR FORCE TRAINING SCHOOL AND BARRACKS. In 1942, the War Department purchased the Stevens Hotel. From caption on reverse: "World's largest hotel enlists for duration … [and] houses thousands of soldiers in training as radio operator-mechanics at the Army Air Forces Technical Training Command's newest radio school. Guests' rooms are army barracks. Famous ballrooms, dining rooms and cocktail lounges are mess halls, classrooms and laboratories." The hotel reopened for civilian guests on November 1, 1943. It is known today as the Chicago Hilton and Towers. (CLC)

THE BLACKSTONE HOTEL [E]. Marshall & Fox, 1908; 636 S. Michigan Avenue (**M4**). The Blackstone's architect, Benjamin Marshall, intended to bring a taste of Paris to Chicago with his design for this building. The hotel was named after Timothy Blackstone, the president of the Illinois Central Railroad Company, who built the hotel to accommodate passengers of his trains. The building's mansard roof no longer sports the large flagpoles and spires that appear in this view. The building is currently undergoing a conversion to condominiums, and its historic spaces, such as the elegant lobby, will be restored. From caption on back: "The World Famous Blackstone is one of Chicago's most prominent and beautiful hotels . . . The Mayfair Room, featuring excellent entertainment, music for dancing and world famous Blackstone food is the meeting place for Chicago's smart social set. Here also is located the unique Balinese Room." (AC)

MICHIGAN AVENUE, LOOKING NORTH FROM THE BLACKSTONE HOTEL. Message from sender: "Dear Aunt Mamie, How are you. We were all in Chicago and enjoyed our visit very much. Will tell you all the sights we saw if you will be sure and come up for Christmas. Send us a card and we will meet you at the depot. Your Loving Cousin, Gertrude G." (VOH-1908)

AUDITORIUM ANNEX [E]. Clinton J. Warren, 1893 and Holabird & Roche, 1902, 1907; 520 S. Michigan Avenue (**M5**). The Auditorium Annex, here with flag saying "The Auditorium," was built as an expansion of the Auditorium Hotel, the building to its right. The two were connected by a marble passageway beneath Congress Parkway called "Peacock Alley," after the famous opera stars and actors who passed through it while performing at the Auditorium Theater. The Auditorium Annex, later known as the Congress Hotel, had its own addition (an "annex to the annex") resulting in the U-shaped structure in this view. (CT)

AUDITORIUM HOTEL AND ANNEX, FINE ARTS BUILDING, AND CHICAGO CLUB. The Auditorium Annex, designed to harmonize with the earlier Auditorium Hotel, repeated the pattern of window groupings and arcades. The hotel's entrance on Michigan Avenue was also similar to that of the Auditorium Hotel. The addition to the Annex omitted the window arcades but retained the pattern created by the bay windows. The Fine Arts Building and Chicago Club appear at the right (pp. 18–19). (1908)

GRAND LOBBY.

GRAND LOBBY OF CONGRESS HOTEL. (v Although much of the interior of the Congress Hotel has been modernized, this lobby remains mostly intact. Changes have been made to the light fixtures and furniture, but the beautiful mosaic designs on the walls and arches above the doorways, as well as the ornate clock that appears here in the archway, remain.) (CT)

JAPANESE TEA ROOM. CONGRESS HOTEL AND ANNEX CHICAGO

JAPANESE TEA ROOM, CONGRESS HOTEL AND ANNEX. The Auditorium Annex was constructed in 1893, the year of the World's Columbian Exposition, and the décor of this room catered to the public's interest in the foreign and exotic. This room no longer exists, but it probably looked out on Michigan Avenue and the lake (note windows and window seats at right). (VOH-1907)

AUDITORIUM BUILDING [E]. Adler & Sullivan, 1887–89; 430 S. Michigan Avenue (**M6**). Adler & Sullivan's success with this ambitious project that combined four buildings in one—hotel, concert hall, office building, and observation tower—secured their position as leaders in the architectural community. The design of the building's exterior, constructed of masonry walls, was influenced by the Marshall Field's Wholesale Store (p. 97). Metal framing was used within. The building has been owned by Roosevelt University since 1946. (v The Roosevelt University lobby occupies the former hotel lobby. Look for the original mosaic floor and stained glass in the stairway between second and third floors.) (VOH)

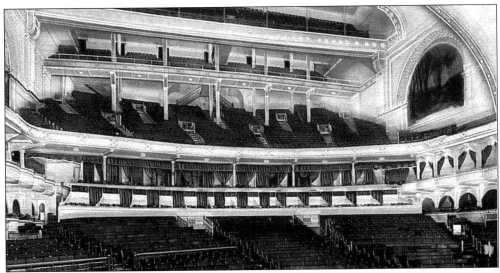

INTERIOR OF AUDITORIUM THEATER. Adler's engineering genius created an acoustically perfect theater that was further enhanced by Sullivan's designs. The theater contained a number of innovations such as extensive use of electric lights and an early form of air conditioning. Part of the theater's lobby was lost when Congress Parkway was widened. Sidewalk arcades were created by carving out interior space from the Auditorium Building and Congress Hotel. (MRS-1916)

102 Auditorium Hotel and Michigan Ave. Chicago, Ill.

VIEW NORTH ON MICHIGAN AVENUE, FROM HARRISON STREET. The Auditorium Annex and Auditorium Hotel are the two large buildings on the left. This slightly later view shows a second southern addition to the Auditorium Annex. (Note that the left half of the "U," shown on page 15, is now eight window bays wider.) The Montgomery Ward Building Tower (pp. 31–32) can be seen in the distance, and the Art Institute is at the right. (SSK-1910)

36 The Studebaker, Chicago, Ill.

THE STUDEBAKER BUILDING [E]. Solon S. Beman, 1885, 1898; 410 S. Michigan Avenue (**M7**). This building originally housed showrooms and assembly shops for the Studebaker Carriage Company. In 1898, three floors were added, theaters and studio space created, and the building became (and remains) the Fine Arts Building. (v A sign above the entrance reads: "All Passes—Art Alone Endures." Inside, plaques identify studios once occupied by Loredo Taft, Frank Lloyd Wright, W.W. Denslow, and L. Frank Baum.) (UP)

CHICAGO CLUB [D]. Burnham & Root, 1887; Southwest corner of Michigan Avenue and Van Buren Street (**M8**). The Art Institute of Chicago hired John Wellborn Root to design this building to replace a smaller building, also by Root, at the corner of Michigan Avenue and Van Buren Street. The rusticated stone and Romanesque style show the influence of H.H. Richardson. One critic commented that the design seemed more suitable for a clubhouse, which, in fact, it became. When the Art Institute moved to its current building, the Chicago Club purchased this building. In 1929, while being remodeled, it collapsed. The site is occupied today by a replacement structure. A portion of the Fine Arts Building and skylights of its top floor studios appear at the left. (FP)

MICHIGAN AVENUE, VIEWED FROM GRANT PARK. This postcard view dramatically illustrates the impact of the architectural developments that occurred in Chicago during the late 1880s and 1890s. With the use of steel-frame construction, the Railway Exchange Building (now the Santa Fe Building) towers over nearby buildings such as the Stratford Hotel, built in 1872. Within a few years, many of the older buildings would be replaced by the structures that make up the famous "Michigan Avenue Streetwall" of today. The buildings shown here, from left to right, are the Auditorium Hotel,

Fine Arts Building, Chicago Club, Victoria Hotel, an unidentified office building, a small perfumery, Karpen Building, Stratford Hotel, Railway Exchange Building, Orchestra Hall, Pullman Building, Peoples Gas, Light and Coke Co. General Offices (not the current Peoples Gas Building, but an earlier one on the same site), two four-story millinery buildings (including a straw hat factory), the Art Institute of Chicago, and, rising above the Art Institute in the distance, the tower of the Montgomery Ward & Co. Building. (VOH-**1909**)

McCormick Building, First Phase [E]. Holabird & Roche, 1910, 1912; 330–332 S. Michigan Avenue (**M9**). The McCormick Building was built for Robert Hall McCormick, nephew of reaper inventor Cyrus McCormick, on the site of the Victoria Hotel (see previous card). The 20-story building was constructed to the full height permitted by city code at that time, and erected in two stages. This postcard depicts the first phase. (v During recent construction work on the Grant Park parking garage across the street, the original coffered ceiling in the lobby collapsed. The elegant gilded ceiling has since been reconstructed.)

McCormick Building, Completed. The perfectly-matching northern addition was completed two years later, on the site of two office buildings (see pp. 20–21 to view buildings previously occupying this location). (GB)

672. Michigan and Jackson Boulevards, Chicago.

STRATFORD HOTEL [D]. W.W. Boyington, 1872; Southwest corner of Michigan Avenue and Jackson Boulevard (**M10**). The Stratford Hotel, in the center of this view, was designed by W.W. Boyington, who was also architect of the Chicago Water Tower. Part of the McCormick Building appears at the far left. Between the McCormick Building and the Stratford Hotel is the extant Karpen Building (1885, architect unknown) and to the right of the Stratford is the Railway Exchange Building. The Stratford Hotel stood until 1922, when construction began on the Straus Building (see below). (A-1913)

CONTINENTAL COMPANIES BUILDING [E]. Graham, Anderson, Probst & White, 1924; 310 S. Michigan Avenue (**M10**). This building, originally the Straus Building, was built on the site of the Stratford Hotel (above) and was one of the first designed after a 1923 zoning law that allowed buildings to exceed 260 feet if setbacks were used. The glass beehive atop the stair-step tower was intended to symbolize thrift, appropriate for the banking company S.W. Straus. Later, this insurance institution occupied the building. (CT-**1944**)

Continental Companies Building
Michigan Ave., at
Jackson Blvd.,
Chicago

RAILWAY EXCHANGE BUILDING [E]. D.H. Burnham & Co., 1904; 224 S. Michigan Avenue (**M11**). The Railway Exchange Building, now known as the Santa Fe Center, once held offices for more than a dozen railroad companies. For many years Daniel Burnham's offices were on the top floor, and it was here he worked on the 1909 Plan of Chicago. The building surrounds a central light well, a device used by Burnham and others to bring light to the interior of buildings. In the 1980s, the second-story skylight above the central lobby was replaced, and a second skylight was added to the top of the building, previously open to the sky. The windows facing the light well, on floors three to seventeen, were removed to create a single large, open, and multi-floored interior space. (v The Chicago Architecture Foundation has offices, exhibit space, and a gift shop on the ground floor.) (PS)

THOMAS ORCHESTRA HALL [E]. D.H. Burnham & Co., 1905; 220 S. Michigan Avenue (**M12**). Theodore Thomas, founder of the Chicago Symphony Orchestra, wished for a more intimate concert hall than its original home, the Auditorium Theater. Burnham was a trustee of the Orchestra Association and, donating his services, designed this Georgian Revival building. Sadly, Thomas died soon after conducting his first concert here. This view depicts the building prior to an inconspicuous one-floor addition by Howard Van Doren Shaw in 1908, which is tucked behind the balustrade at the top. (ACB-1908)

ART INSTITUTE OF CHICAGO [E]. Shepley, Rutan & Coolidge, 1893; Michigan at Adams Street (**M13**). Built for the 1893 World's Columbian Exposition, this structure was first used to house international congresses, such as the World's Parliament of Religions, which assembled in Chicago in conjunction with the World's Fair. The Art Institute of Chicago moved here from their previous location (see p. 19) after the conclusion of the World's Columbian Exposition. The building has since undergone numerous expansions. (SHK-1906)

MCKINLOCK MEMORIAL COURT, ART INSTITUTE OF CHICAGO. Constructed in 1924, this interior courtyard was designed by the firm of Coolidge & Hodgdon. During the summer months the setting is used for outdoor dining and jazz concerts. This view of Michigan Avenue buildings is now blocked by second story galleries, which surround the courtyard. (MRS)

Michigan Avenue, showing Pullman Bldg., Peoples Gas Bldg. Lakeview Bldg., Illinois Athletic Club, Monroe Bldg. and University Club, Chicago.

PULLMAN BUILDING AND PEOPLES GAS BUILDING. The turreted Romanesque Revival building on the left is the **Pullman Building** [**D**] [Solon S. Beman, 1884; 79 E. Adams Street (**M14**)]. Constructed of brick and granite, this building was nicknamed the "Pullman Hive" and was architect Beman's first building in downtown Chicago. It was one of the first tall commercial buildings on Michigan Avenue and the mixed-use structure contained offices, apartments, and one of the first restaurants in the city with a view—The Tip Top Inn. The Pullman Building was demolished in 1956, and the Borg-Warner Building, completed in 1958, stands on the site today. To the right of the Pullman Building is the **Peoples Gas Building** [**E**] [D.H. Burnham & Co., 1910; 122 S. Michigan Avenue (**M15**)]. The eclectic façade combines Classical, Egyptian, Renaissance, and Baroque elements. (MRS-**1914**)

INTERIOR PEOPLES GAS

LOBBY OF PEOPLES GAS BUILDING. The interior of the Peoples Gas Building continued the use of the classical motifs found on the exterior, such as the Ionic columns surrounding this sky-lit lobby. (v Although this lobby no longer remains, the marble walls and elevator doorways visible behind the columns appear to be the same as those in the building today.) (VOH)

MICHIGAN AVENUE, LOOKING SOUTH FROM MONROE STREET. The term "cliff-dwellers" was first used by Chicago writer Henry Fuller to describe the office workers of Chicago, and the buildings they occupied, in his novel *Cliff-Dwellers* (1893). The analogy can be understood when viewing the sheer wall of buildings depicted here. This section of Michigan Avenue, facing Grant Park and once nearly on the edge of Lake Michigan, is often referred to as the "Michigan Avenue Cliff," or the "Michigan Avenue Streetwall." (GB)

MICHIGAN AVENUE, LOOKING NORTH FROM THE ART INSTITUTE. This view looks north on Michigan Avenue from the Art Institute. The Peoples Gas Building appears at the left. (VOH-1917)

MUNICIPAL COURTS BUILDING AND ILLINOIS ATHLETIC CLUB. THE **MUNICIPAL COURTS BUILDING [E]**, [Jenney, Mundie & Jensen, 1906, 1912; 116 S. Michigan Avenue (**M16**)], also known as the Lake View Building, is the narrow building on the left. It provided temporary courtroom space when the Chicago City Hall and Courthouse were rebuilt (see p. 84). The **Illinois Athletic Club [E]** [Barnett, Haynes & Barnett, 1908; 112 S. Michigan Avenue (**M17**)] features a frieze of chariots and athletic contestants just below the original cornice, now located beneath six floors added in 1985. (VOH-1911)

PEOPLES GAS BLDG. LAKE VIEW BLDG. ILLINOIS ATHLETIC CLUB MONROE BLDG. UNIVERSITY CLUB

A MAGNIFICENT ROW ON MICHIGAN AVE., CHICAGO   Copyright 1912, V. O. Hammon, Pub. Co.

"A Magnificent Row on Michigan Avenue." The gabled building in the center is the **Monroe Building** [**E**] [Holabird & Roche, 1912; 104 S. Michigan Avenue (**M18**)]. The Monroe Building's height and roofline were designed to harmonize with the University Club, at right. (v The lobby of the Monroe Building continues the Italian Renaissance styling of the exterior, and features beautiful vaulted ceilings and Rookwood tiles.) (VOH-**1912**)

University Club, Chicago.

University Club [E]. Holabird & Roche, 1909; 76 E. Monroe Street (**M19**). The gargoyles, crockets, and other Gothic details on this structure bring to mind buildings at the University of Chicago campus, six miles south. Their application here, to a skyscraper, is surprisingly effective. Beneath the gabled roof is a three-story dining room. (IW)

29

MILLINERY BUILDING (GAGE BUILDING) [E]. Holabird & Roche, Louis Sullivan, 1899; 18 S. Michigan Avenue (**M20**). The Michigan Avenue buildings facing Grant Park were assured unblocked light from the east, which made the location attractive to the millinery trade, whose employees required well-lit facilities. This building and two to the south were designed by the firm of Holabird & Roche. The façade of this building, however, was the work of Louis Sullivan. Here the building is shown prior to a 1902 addition that added four stories (compare to postcard at right). Following the addition, the two foliate "clasps" at the top were replaced, but the additional height made them somewhat out of scale. Ornate cast ironwork that once decorated the building at the street level can be seen here. (KK)

CHICAGO ATHLETIC ASSOCIATION BUILDING [E]. Henry Ives Cobb, 1893; 12 S. Michigan Avenue (**M21**). This building was designed for one of the largest athletic clubs in Chicago, and its delicate brickwork displays many Venetian Gothic details. Compare its cornice height, on this and the previous card, to that of the Millinery Building (to the left) before and after its addition. (VOH)

VIEW OF MILLINERY BUILDING, CHICAGO ATHLETIC ASSOCIATION, AND MONTGOMERY WARD BUILDING. In this view, standing to the right of the Chicago Athletic Association Building is an eight-story building known as the Willoughby Building. In 1929, it was replaced by the "Willoughby Tower" (see next page). To its right are the Montgomery Ward Building and the Chicago Public Library (pages 32–33). The low building at right edge was a temporary post office. (RTS)

WILLOUGHBY TOWER AND MONTGOMERY WARD BUILDING ("TOWER BUILDING").
The tall building on the left is the **Willoughby Tower** [E] [Samuel N. Crowen & Assoc., 1929; 8 S. Michigan Avenue (M22)]. On the right is the **Montgomery Ward & Co. Building** [E] [Richard E. Schmidt, 1899 and Holabird & Roche, 1923; 6 N. Michigan Avenue (M23)]. At one time, paying a visit to the Tower Building's observation deck and mailing a postcard with verse were almost obligatory activities for every Chicago visitor. The following poem, sent in 1906, is typical: "Sing a Song of Post Cards, This is from the Sky—Four and twenty Stories, How is that for High!!!" Holabird & Roche's four-story addition, built on each side of the tower, appears in this view (compare to pages 2, 31). (v Seeing the building here, beside the still existing Willoughby Tower, helps one imagine the original height of the Montgomery Ward Tower, the upper section of which was removed in 1947.) (MRS-1933)

MICHIGAN BOULEVARD BUILDING [E].
Jarvis Hunt, 1914; 30 N. Michigan Avenue (M24). The Michigan Boulevard Building stands just south of the Chicago Public Library, on what was once the site of a firehouse. This view shows the building at its original 15-story height; Hunt added six more stories in 1923. Caption on back reads: "The Michigan Boulevard Building is located at the corner of Washington St. and Michigan Boulevard and is the latest of the many modern skyscrapers that overlook the lake on Michigan Boulevard. It is strictly fireproof, being built entirely of sandstone and steel." (MRS-1916)

CHICAGO PUBLIC LIBRARY [E]. Shepley, Rutan & Coolidge, 1897; 78 E. Washington Street (**M25**). The Chicago Public Library operated as Chicago's main library from 1897 until 1991, when the Harold Washington Library was opened. Within are exquisite mosaic floors and ceilings, two magnificent stained-glass domes, and marble staircases. The building now houses the Chicago Cultural Center and provides exhibit and performance space, a visitor center, and permanent museums. (HCL)

Interior of Public Library, Chicago.

CIRCULATION DESK, CHICAGO PUBLIC LIBRARY. Thought to be the world's largest Tiffany dome, this glass ceiling features a fish scale pattern with astrological signs decorating the center. The circulation desk, straight ahead in this view, was removed in 1977 when the space was converted into Preston Bradley Hall. From the message on back: "... The little Dutch bonnets are fine for motoring. We are going down to shop and see the styles... ." (v On this room's mosaic walls are printers' symbols, names of famous writers, quotations, and natural designs.) (1910)

PERISTYLE AND VIEW SOUTH FROM RANDOLPH STREET. Standing at this spot today, Millennium Park and its Bank One Promenade, constructed above the railroad tracks shown here, stretch out before you. On your left is the new Frank Gehry-designed music pavilion and at your right, a nearly full-size replica of this peristyle, erected in 1917. The presence of the peristyle and the height of the Michigan Boulevard Building (page 32) date this image to between 1917 and 1923. (MRS)

VIEW NORTH FROM PERISTYLE. Several skyscrapers built during the 1920s along North Michigan Avenue appear here. They are, from right to left, the Tribune Tower, 333 Building with Bell Building in front of it, the belvedere of the London Guarantee & Accident Building, the Carbide and Carbon Building, and at the left edge, the **John Crerar Library [D]** [Holabird & Roche, 1920; Northwest corner of Michigan and Randolph (**M26**)], now site of the Smurfit-Stone Building. (MRS-**1933**)

Two

WABASH AVENUE

Wabash Avenue encompassed several distinct districts along its length. At the north end was Jeweler's Row, shown below. A medical district stretched between Wabash and Dearborn Street, from Madison Street north to South Water Street (now Wacker Drive). The Pittsfield Building and Garland Building, included here, were buildings developed for and originally occupied by the medical professions. At the south end, between Congress and Adams Street, was "Piano Row." The Cable and Steger Buildings, shown in this chapter, were built for piano companies of the same name. Nearby office buildings were occupied by musical colleges and vocal and instrumental instructors. In 1897, Wabash Avenue was permanently impacted by the construction of the Union Loop Elevated Train.

WABASH AVENUE, LOOKING NORTHWEST FROM MONROE STREET. This block of Wabash Avenue, part of "Jeweler's Row," still retains most of the buildings shown here. Looking across the elevated tracks, the tall building, second from the left, that rises out of view is the **Thomas Church Building** (or **Carson Pirie Scott Annex**) [E] [Hill & Woltersdorf, 1903; 32 S. Wabash Avenue (**W1**)]. The next two buildings to the right also still stand, although minus their peaked cornices. A sign painted on its side identifies the **Silversmith Building** [E] [D.H. Burnham & Co., 1897; 10 S. Wabash Avenue (**W2**)], once occupied by jewelers and silversmiths. It features a beautiful deep green terra-cotta and brick façade and is now a hotel. To the right of the Silversmith Building is the Heyworth Building and in the right foreground, is the Powers Building (see page 37 for both). (VOH)

Wabash Avenue

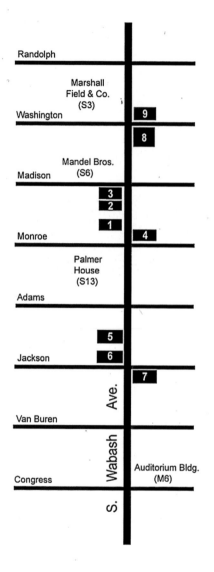

W 1. Thomas Church Building
W 2. Silversmith Building
W 3. Heyworth Building
W 4. Powers Building
W 5. McClurg Building
W 6. Steger Building
W 7. Cable Building
W 8. Pittsfield Building
W 9. Garland Building

HEYWORTH BUILDING [E]. D.H. Burnham & Co., 1905; 8 S. Wabash Avenue (**W3**). The Heyworth Building was developed by a wholesale jeweler. He named the building after his son-in-law, Lawrence Heyworth, who had supervised its construction. The first occupants were jewelers and watchmakers. A plaque near the entrance reads: "This distinctive structure combines the structurally expressive character of the Chicago School with the decorative appearance of traditional masonry architecture . . . The building's tapestry-like ornament is influenced by the adjacent Carson Pirie Scott department store by Louis Sullivan." It has recently undergone an extensive renovation including the rebuilding of its missing cornice. (FP)

POWERS BUILDING (SECOND CHAMPLAIN BUILDING) [E]. Holabird & Roche, 1903; 37 S. Wabash Avenue (**W4**). The trademark features of Holabird & Roche, repeated in much of their work between 1895 and 1910, are visible here: wide Chicago windows, continuous piers, recessed spandrels, and clean lines. Architect Ludwig Mies van der Rohe once had offices in this building. (KK)

McClurg Building [E]. Holabird & Roche, 1899; 218 S. Wabash Avenue (**W5**). This important building illustrates the qualities that made the Chicago School of architecture, and its gifted proponents, Holabird & Roche, famous. The simple façade is composed of a grid of thin spandrels and piers which articulates the steel-frame structure underlying it. The building once housed the McClurg Booksellers and Stationers (note signs). It has also been known as the Pakula Building, Crown Building, and Ayer Building. (BS-1909)

STEGER BUILDING [E]. Marshall & Fox, 1909; 28 E. Jackson Boulevard. (**W6**). The Steger Building was located on "Piano Row" and housed the offices and showroom of the Steger Piano Company. The pianos were manufactured at the company factory in Steger, Illinois, 29 miles away. The McClurg Building can be seen at the right. (v Look for the name "Steger" above the entrance on Jackson Boulevard.) (VOH-**1912**)

VIEW NORTH ON WABASH AVENUE FROM VAN BUREN STREET. More of "Piano Row" appears on this postcard. The tallest building on the right is the **Cable Building [D]** [Holabird & Roche, 1898; southeast corner of Wabash and Jackson. (**W7**)], demolished in 1961. Its tall and clean appearance presents a striking contrast to the low and ornate masonry buildings nearby, probably constructed 10 to 20 years earlier. A sign identifies it as "Cable Pianos"; signs for other piano dealers can be seen on the left. Note "McClurg," written vertically on the side of the McClurg Building, in the distance on the left. (VOH-1912)

39

PITTSFIELD BUILDING [E]. Graham, Anderson, Probst & White, 1927; 55 E. Washington Street (**W8**). For a short time the Pittsfield Building was Chicago's tallest structure. Its original occupants were mainly physicians, dentists, and jewelers. This view from Grant Park includes, on the left, the Michigan Boulevard Building, depicted here after a six floor addition (compare to postcard on p. 32). The Chicago Public Library appears in the right foreground, and behind the library is the Garland Building (see next). (v The Pittsfield still retains its original lobby, elevators, and charming five-story interior shopping arcade.) (MRS-1928)

GARLAND BUILDING [E]. Christian A. Eckstorm, 1914; 111 N. Wabash Avenue, 59 E. Washington Street (**W9**). This view from the southeast shows the Washington Street entrance to the Garland Building. The structure was 16 stories high when first built; six more floors were added in 1922. The Garland Building currently houses about 250 medical, dental, and counseling offices. A condominium tower, "Heritage at Millennium Park," is now under construction just to the north of the Garland Building. Façades of four of the seven Wabash Avenue buildings previously on the site were saved and are being incorporated into the new structure. (MRS-1920)

Three

STATE STREET

State Street is one of the most famous shopping streets in the world. It was the brainchild of Potter Palmer who, in 1863, built the first department store here; it became Marshall Field's & Company. Others copied his successful operation, and soon department stores lined State Street south to Congress. Postcards of eight of these stores are included in this chapter. From *The Souvenir Guide to Chicago* (1912): "No part of Chicago has been more frequently described than its big store district, and of no part does description seem more inadequate. Take your stand at any point on State St. . . . and you can see nine of the largest retail stores in the world, some of them covering almost an entire square. . . . A journey up this street is a never-to-be-forgotten event. Each of the large stores has its rest room, often magnificently furnished and usually well supplied with books, magazines, newspapers, and writing materials. Connected with the rest rooms are finely appointed toilet rooms. High-class restaurants, for the accommodation of patrons, are to be found in nearly all of these large establishments."

A VIEW OF STATE STREET, LOOKING NORTH FROM MADISON. This view looks north from the intersection of State and Madison Streets, "the busiest corner in the world." This was the heart of Chicago's shopping district and three department stores—Mandel Brothers, Marshall Field & Co., and Boston Store—appear here. (RTS)

State Street

Randolph

1

2

3

Washington

7   4

5

8   6

Madison

10

9

11

Monroe

12

13

Adams

14

15

S. State Street

Jackson

16

Van Buren

Harold
Washington
Library

17

Congress

N
↑

S1. Masonic Temple
S2. Central Music Hall
S3. Marshall Field & Co. Store
S4. Columbus Memorial Building
S5. Stevens Building
S6. Mandel Brothers
S7. Reliance Building
S8. Boston Store (Sears)
S9. Carson Pirie Scott & Co. Store
S10. Chicago Building
S11. Majestic Building
S12. Mentor Building
S13. Palmer House
S14. The Fair
S15. Republic Building
S16. Rothschild & Co. Store
     (DePaul Center)
S17. Siegel, Cooper & Co. Store
     (Robert Morris Center)

MASONIC TEMPLE AND CENTRAL MUSIC HALL. The **Masonic Temple** [D] [Burnham & Root, 1891–92; northeast corner of State and Randolph Streets (**S1**)], rose to the astonishing height of 22 stories, which, when it was completed in 1892, easily made it the world's tallest building. With a restaurant seating 2,000, a rooftop conservatory, a theater, and 14 elevators, the building attracted much attention. Many visitors to the 1893 World's Columbian Exposition found it of greater interest than the fair's Beaux Arts exhibition halls. The Masonic Temple was demolished in 1939 leaving a void that can be sensed to this day. In 1987, it made a reappearance of sorts with Philip Johnson's homage to it in his design of the postmodern office building at 190 South La Salle Street. The cupola-topped structure at the right is the **Central Music Hall** [D] [Dankmar Adler, 1879; southeast corner of State and Randolph Streets (**S2**)]. It was Dankmar Adler's first independent commission, and his design solution to the building's multiple uses, and the hall's outstanding acoustics, foreshadowed Adler and Sullivan's later triumph with the Auditorium Building (see page 17). Adler wanted the Central Music Hall, more than any other, to remain as a memorial to his work. Sadly, it was demolished in 1901 when the northwest block of the Marshall Field's & Co. store was built on the site. (WGM)

VIEW EAST FROM TOP OF MASONIC TEMPLE. Looking east from the observation deck at the top of the Masonic Temple, visitors could see the mouth of the Chicago River (where the plume of smoke and boat appear, at the left) and the freight yards and railroad tracks that, well into the 1960s, occupied this area south of the Chicago River. The Chicago Yacht Club is visible at the lake's edge, in the center of the view. (ACB)

VIEW NORTH FROM TOP OF MASONIC TEMPLE. Looking north, in the foreground, the Chicago River and the State Street Bridge were visible. Further up State Street, on the right, was the still-standing Holy Name Cathedral (note spire in distance). The white building on the left edge, the Cook County Criminal Courts Building, also still stands. The Newberry Library can be seen in the distance. (VOH)

MARSHALL FIELD & CO. STORE [E]. 1892–1907; 111 N. State Street (**S3**). Through the years this department store, an amalgam of structures, has been added to and remodeled in sections. This view depicts the store in transition to the current structure, and three distinct buildings are visible. Behind, to the right, is the southeast corner and earliest building (1892, Charles Atwood, D.H. Burnham & Co.). On the left, just to the right of the Masonic Temple, is the northwest building

(1902, D.H. Burnham & Co.) that replaced the Central Music Hall (p. 43). The building on the southwest corner, directly facing the photographer, no longer exists. In 1907, it was replaced by the still-standing building, which seamlessly matches the 1902 building to its left. (HCL)

"LIGHT SHAFT IN MARSHALL FIELD & CO.'S STORE." This postcard depicts a light well that illuminated the interior of the northwest section of Marshall Field's. It was covered by clear glass, and this open, balconied space remains mostly unchanged today. (v An exquisite mosaic dome designed by Louis Comfort Tiffany in 1907, and large Tiffany lamps, top a similar space in the southwest building.) (VOH-1911)

LIGHT SHAFT IN MARSHALL FIELD & CO.'S STORE, CHICAGO.

COLUMBUS MEMORIAL BUILDING [D]. W.W. Boyington, 1892; 31 N. State Street (**S4**). The name and theme of this top-heavy-appearing building were inspired by the World's Columbian Exposition, under construction simultaneously with this structure. A statue of Columbus stood in a niche above the State Street entrance, and mosaic floors and wall panels within depicted his ships and details from his life. The building was originally occupied almost exclusively by jewelers and physicians. It was demolished in 1959. (CT-1907)

STATE STREET, BETWEEN WASHINGTON AND MADISON STREETS. Probably taken about 10 years after the previous photograph, this view shows the Columbus Memorial Building's new neighbors to the south. The **Stevens Building [E]** [D.H. Burnham & Co., 1912; 17 N. State Street (**S5**)] housed the Stevens Department Store on the lower seven floors. Smaller retailers filled the 11 floors above. **Mandel Brothers [E]** [Holabird & Roche, 1912; 1 N. State Street (**S6**)] was a large department store that, like Marshall Field & Co., underwent numerous expansions and remodelings. The cornices on these two buildings are different today, but otherwise the Stevens and Mandel Brothers buildings look largely the same as here. The sender writes: "I have seen no snow since leaving home—Nice weather, warm and green grass here. Quite a burg too." (VOH-1918)

RELIANCE BUILDING [E]. Burnham & Root, 1891; Charles Atwood of D.H. Burnham & Co., 1895; 32 N. State Street (**S7**). The Reliance Building is one of Chicago's finest early skyscrapers. It is also a wonderfully successful example of preservation and reuse. The base of the Reliance Building, designed by Burnham & Root, was constructed four years before the rest of the building. A building already on the site was lifted and the Reliance base was erected beneath it. Four years later, after the older building was demolished, the Reliance Building's upper floors, designed by Charles Atwood, were erected at a remarkable rate, using for the first time in a significant way, "Chicago construction." After 100 years of use, restoration of the badly deteriorated building was begun in 1994. It was completed in 1999, and the remodeled building now houses the Hotel Burnham and Atwood Café. (WGM)

Chicago, Ill. 874. State street looking North.

Thank you for the pretty Christmas

RELIANCE BUILDING AND STATE STREET, LOOKING NORTH. This postcard bears an unusual message, sent in 1908. It begins, in the official message area, with pleasantries. "Thank you for the pretty Christmas card. Have you very much snow?" It continues across the image area with: "There's no ice nor snow here in Chicago. I have been out of work since Jan 1. So many people are walking the streets idle, having been laid off. There are every day so many tramps at our door we are afraid to open it. Regards from Minnie." (PS-1908)

Boston Store, Chicago, Ill.

BOSTON STORE (ORIGINAL CHAMPLAIN BUILDING), FROM THE NORTHEAST [D]. Holabird & Roche, 1894; northwest corner of State and Madison (**S8**). The building on the left was an 1894 addition to the Boston Store structure on the right. Although a fine Chicago School commercial building, it was demolished in 1916 after only 22 years of service, and an even larger Boston Store, also designed by Holabird & Roche, was erected on the site. Signs on the building at right read: "Cash Merchandise. Staples & Fancy Groceries. Furniture, Stoves & Bedding. Clothing, Hats, Caps, Boots & Shoes. Upholstery, Millinery." (AH-1908)

BOSTON STORE, FROM THE SOUTHEAST [E]. Holabird & Roche, 1917; 2 N. State Street (**S8**). This somewhat imaginary view eliminated the foreground buildings and gave the impression that the new Boston Store faced a large piazza. Note its observation tower, the Reliance Building at right and the La Salle Hotel (page 104) at the left edge. Today the building is occupied by Sears. (v Looking up at the building from the southeast corner of State and Washington, it's possible to see the words "Boston Store" painted near the top.) (MRS)

MANDEL BROTHERS TRIPTYCH: VIEWS OF STATE STREET [D] AND ANNEX (MADISON AND WABASH) [E]. This postcard predates the view on page 46 (i.e., this "State St. Front" is an earlier building). The "Madison St. Front" and "Wabash Av. Front" views show the Mandel Brothers Annex, designed by Holabird & Roche in 1900, before and after a 1905 addition of two stories. The postcard reads: "Chicago—Dec. 1905. Dear Madam: Our new dressmaking parlors, 9th floor, Wabash Ave., afford unsurpassed facilities for the construction of artistic costumes, street dresses and tailored gowns. Our tailors and modistes are superbly skilled and strikingly original. Every detail of both daylight and artificial light effects may be studied in especially constructed fitting rooms. Very respectfully, Mandel Brothers." (1905)

MANDEL BROTHERS "HIGH BUILDING," AT CORNER OF STATE AND MADISON. Columbus Memorial Building and Marshall Field's appear in the distance. On back: "1-17-1910. Hello Rosie: Well how are all of you folks out there. I'm all O.K. at my cousin's drug store in Chicago. Say I was out skating Tues. night and Fri. Sat. & Sun. afternoon & Sat. I went in the afternoon & night both so I had about enough skating. There were about 500 or so on the ice at one time & about a 100 in the building & outside watching on Sun. Your Friend Albert. I seen your Pop on the same train that I came up on." (R-1910)

"BUSIEST CORNER IN THE WORLD." The intersection of Madison and State Streets, long touted as the "busiest corner in the world," is also the baseline for the numbering of Chicago street addresses. In this view, looking east on Madison, the earlier Mandel Brothers store appears on the left. Behind it, to the right, is the modern-looking Mandel Brothers Annex. At right is the ornate and beautiful corner entrance to Carson Pirie Scott & Co. (see next). (VOH)

CARSON PIRIE SCOTT & CO. [E]. Louis H. Sullivan, 1899, 1903; 1 S. State Street (**S9**). This building, one of the most famous early skyscrapers, became a prototype for the modern department store. Louis Sullivan's use of steel-frame construction, applied here for the first time to a large retail structure, allowed for maximum display area for merchandise and an abundance of natural light, which flooded through the large glass windows sheathing the exterior. Sullivan's design, though largely of horizontal lines, focused on the corner entrance and a vertical corner tower which still retains his ornate ironwork. The cornice, removed long ago, is now being rebuilt. (FP)

Chicago

Chicago Savings Bank Bldg.

We leave Chicago at 11 to night

CHICAGO BUILDING (CHICAGO SAVINGS BANK BUILDING) [E]. Holabird & Roche, 1904; 7 W. Madison Street (**S10**). The Chicago Building epitomizes the Chicago School of architecture and is one of its most intact early examples. The rare original cornice is noteworthy. A jog in State Street at Madison allows for a less obstructed view of both the north and east façades with their two types of Chicago windows; flat along State Street and alternating flat, and projecting bay, along Madison. In 1997, the building was converted into residences by the School of the Art Institute of Chicago. The McVickers Theater (pages 75–76) is the building to the right of the Chicago Building. (CT-1907)

**MAJESTIC BUILDING (MAJESTIC THEATER)
[E].** Edmund R. Krause, 1905; 16–22
W. Monroe Street (**S11**). "This structure,
erected in 1906, is 20 stories high and having
a very narrow front is a striking specimen
of skyscraper architecture. It houses many
offices and is without doubt one of the
finest vaudeville houses in the world. The
theater has a beautiful marble entrance and
the highly ornamental foyer is decorated
with fine paintings." (*A Guide to the City of
Chicago,* 1909.) A restoration of the building
is planned to be completed within the next
two years and will return the lobby to its
original size and splendor. (CT-1908)

**MAJESTIC BUILDING, LOOKING WEST FROM
STATE STREET.** The Majestic Theater, now
known as the Shubert Theater, opened on
New Year's Day 1906 and was an instant
tourist attraction. In its heyday it offered 12
to 15 continuously running vaudeville acts a
day, six days a week that starred performers
such as Lily Langtry and Harry Houdini.
It was closed for 15 years during the Great
Depression. Lee and J.J. Shubert purchased the
building in 1945 and renamed the theater the
Sam Shubert Theater; the office portion has
kept the name Majestic Building. (UP-1910)

53

CITY AND LAKE FROM MAJESTIC BUILDING, CHICAGO
(WITH CIRCUIT CAMERA)
No. 1331. V. O. Hammon Pub. Co., Chicago

VIEW EAST FROM TOP OF MAJESTIC BUILDING. Recognizable buildings are, from left to right: Chicago Building (at left edge), Mandel Bros., Carson Pirie Scott, Heyworth Building, Montgomery Ward Building, Mentor Building (center foreground), Illinois Athletic Association, Pullman Building, Railway Exchange Building, and Palmer House (right foreground). This high vantage point provides an interesting look at the rooftops of the Carson Pirie Scott store, Mentor Building, and the Palmer House (left to right in foreground). (VOH-**1907**)

Mentor Building, Chicago.

MENTOR BUILDING [E]. Howard Van Doren Shaw, 1906; 39 S. State Street (**S12**).
The Mentor Building is the only skyscraper designed by Howard Van Doren Shaw, who was mostly known for residential designs. The building was faced with gray bricks and accented with cream-colored terra-cotta trim. Its tripartite organization included a four-story base with large display windows, which in this view, are filled with dresses on the second and third floors. A corner of the Palmer House appears at right.

PALMER HOUSE [D]. John M. Van Osdel, 1872–73; southeast corner of Monroe and State Streets (**S13**). A Palmer House has stood at this location since 1871, when the hotel moved here from its original location. Two weeks after the opening of the new Palmer House, it was burned to the ground by the Chicago Fire. This postcard depicts the third Palmer House, which opened the following year. Built in the Second Empire style popular during this period, the building is typical of much of Chicago's post-fire construction. The awning-covered entrance at left, on Monroe Street, was the "Ladies Entrance." The building was demolished in 1925 to make way for the fourth, and current, Palmer House. (HCL)

PALMER HOUSE [E]. Holabird & Roche, 1927; 17 E. Monroe Street (**S13**). This postcard depicts the current Palmer House. Designed by the same architects as the slightly larger Stevens Hotel (see p. 13), the Palmer House has similar narrow towers which surround light wells.

The EMPIRE ROOM of the PALMER HOUSE in CHICAGO

Palmer House   Chicago, Illinois   57

EMPIRE ROOM, PALMER HOUSE [E].
For decades this 350-seat room showcased the most popular musicians and singers in the entertainment industry. The room opened in 1933 in time for the 1933–34 Chicago World's Fair. Through the years headliners included Frank Sinatra, Tony Bennett, Harry Belafonte, Edith Piaf, Ella Fitzgerald, Jimmy Durante, Judy Garland, Jack Benny, and Liberace. From caption on back: "The Empire Room . . . is famous for its brilliant revues and name bands presented at dinner and supper nightly. Concert ensemble at luncheon daily." (CT)

PALMER HOUSE. Compare this Art Deco rendering of the current Palmer House to the more realistic portrayal on the previous page. (CGC)

View North at State and Adams Streets. The House of Peacock, Chicago's first jewelry store, opened in 1837 on Lake Street. By the time this postcard was published, the store had moved to the corner of State and Adams Streets and was renamed "C.D. Peacock." The large building on the left is The Fair. (v In 1927, C.D. Peacock moved to the north end of the block where its beautiful brass peacock doors remain, at the corner of State and Monroe Streets.) (PS-1906)

The Fair [D]. William Le Baron Jenney, 1891; northwest corner of State and Adams Streets (S14). The Fair was another colossal department store on State Street. A large boxy structure of warehouse construction, The Fair's elevations, despite some distracting ornamentation, expressed the underlying steel and iron framing. The building was remodeled in 1965 and became Montgomery Ward's flagship store. In 1985, the building was demolished and some of its foundation was utilized in the construction of Bank One Center, now on the site. The building visible just beyond The Fair, on the left, is the Marquette Building (see page 74). (A)

The Republic Bldg. with The States Restaurant, Chicago.

REPUBLIC BUILDING [D]. Holabird & Roche, 1905, 1909; 209 S. State Street (**S15**). This photograph shows the Republic Building at its original 12-story height. In 1909, an additional seven stories were added. With its crisp lines and large windows, historian Carl Condit considered it "the cleanest and lightest of all Holabird & Roche designs" and its demolition in 1961, "a major civic loss." (KK)

VIEW NORTH ON STATE STREET, FROM JACKSON BOULEVARD. This street scene includes the Republic Building, again prior to 1909 addition, to the left of the American flag (note sign). Also visible is the Mentor Building (the tall building to the left of the Republic) and the McClurg Building (the top of its rear elevation appears to the right of the American flag).

ROTHSCHILD & CO. STORE [E]. Holabird & Roche, 1912; 333 S. State Street (**S16**). Built on the site of an earlier Rothschild store, this 1912 structure, now the DePaul Center, filled almost the entire block between Jackson Boulevard and Van Buren Street. (A narrow building once stood between it and Jackson Boulevard.) Two of the building's most distinguishing features, the large deep cornice and two-story arcade display windows, are visible here. (v "R"s, for Rothschild, are still visible on the façade today.) (MRS-1915)

SIEGEL, COOPER AND COMPANY STORE (SECOND LEITER BUILDING) [E]. William Le Baron Jenney, 1891; 403 S. State Street (**S17**). This department store building, directly south of Rothschild & Co., is appreciated today for its almost modern-appearing exterior, which was one of the first to clearly express the underlying steel skeleton. Also significant was Jenney's use of steel and iron framing throughout. This allowed for larger windows and fewer interior supports and created the flexible and well-illuminated interior space the client, Levi Z. Leiter, desired. Occupied for many years by Siegel, Cooper and Co., the building later housed the Leiter Shops, then Sears, Roebuck & Co. The building at left is an earlier Rothschild & Co. Store and the tower at the card's right edge is part of the Auditorium Building. Message on back: "Sept. 13, 1911, Dear Cousin: I am still alive, hope you are all the same. I am in Chicago now. My Brother is here with me. How is everybody in Saginaw? I am just going home for supper now. With love to you all, Your Cousin Laurence. Isn't this store a small one? How is your Ma and Pa? Answer soon." (IW-1911)

Four

DEARBORN STREET

Because many of the city's earliest large office buildings were constructed along the south end of Dearborn Street it became known as Chicago's skyscraper district (see below). One of these, the Manhattan Building, was built in time to wow the visitors attending the 1893 World's Columbian Exposition, who called the building Hercules. It and the famous Monadnock Building are part of a surviving group of early skyscrapers erected here in the 1890s. North of the Monadnock stood a lavish domed Federal Building (well represented by postcards included in this chapter), demolished in 1965, and further north, the beautiful Marquette Building. The Marquette Building still stands but most other nearby buildings have been lost. Theaters were located at the north end, especially along Randolph Street. The Schiller Building (with the Garrick Theater), Woods Theater, and the McVickers Theater have all been demolished but other theaters remain and the area is still known as Chicago's Theater District.

SKY-SCRAPER DISTRICT OF CHICAGO.

"SKY-SCRAPER DISTRICT OF CHICAGO." In this view, looking west on Jackson Boulevard, the buildings of Dearborn Street tower above the older buildings in the foreground. They are, from left to right, the Monadnock Building, Great Northern Theater & Hotel (the U-shaped building group), Marquette Building, and The Fair. (ECK-1907)

61

Dearborn Street

Randolph | 18 | 19 | 20
Daley Center | 17 | 16
Washington
15
Boston Store (S8)
Madison
13 | 14
Monroe | 12
11
10
9 | The Fair (S14)
Adams
8 | Quincy Ct. | 6 | 7
Jackson
5
Van Buren | 4
3
2 | Harold Washington Library
Congress | 1

S. Dearborn St.

Plymouth Ct.

N ↑

D1. Manhattan Building
D2. Plymouth Building
D3. Old Colony Building
D4. Fisher Building
D5. Monadnock Building
D6. Great Northern Hotel
D7. Hotel Majestic
D8. Federal Building and Post Office
D9. Marquette Building
D10. Adams Express Co.
D11. Commercial National Bank
D12. First National Bank Building
D13. Tribune Building
D14. McVickers Theater
D15. Portland Block
D16. Chemical Bank Building
D17. Unity Building
D18. Schiller Building
D19. Borden Block; Woods Theater
D20. Delaware Building

VIEW NORTH ON DEARBORN STREET, SOUTH OF VAN BUREN. This photograph depicts the early skyscrapers of the 400 block of South Dearborn Street. Fortunately, all are still standing. They are, from right to left, the Manhattan Building, Plymouth Building, Old Colony Building, and beyond the elevated train station on Van Buren Street, Fisher Building. The Manhattan Building, at 16 stories, was briefly the world's tallest building. The sender's message included this observation: "Looks like a place where some Biz was being done." (IW-1910)

TALL BUILDINGS AT PLYMOUTH PLACE, CHICAGO.

"TALL BUILDINGS AT PLYMOUTH PLACE." This view, looking north on Plymouth Court, depicts the opposite side (east façade) of the buildings shown on the previous postcard. At the left is the Como Building (demolished in 1938 to make way for the extension of Congress Parkway). Next is the **Manhattan Building [E]** [William Le Baron Jenney, 1891; 431 S. Dearborn Street (**D1**)], the oldest steel-frame building remaining in Chicago. To the right of the Manhattan is the 10-story **Plymouth Building [E]** [Simeon B Eisendrath, 1899; 417 S. Dearborn Street (**D2**)]. Beyond the Plymouth Building are the Old Colony and Fisher Buildings. (v Look for remnants of the Como Building's walls on the south end of the Manhattan Building. In the lobby of the Plymouth Building, off Dearborn, is an original marble staircase with Sullivanesque cast-iron banister; the building's Plymouth Court façade features ornate ironwork on the first and second floors.) (VOH)

OLD COLONY BUILDING, CHICAGO, ILL.

OLD COLONY BUILDING [E]. Holabird & Roche, 1894; 407 S. Dearborn Street (**D3**). A Boston developer named this building after the first English colony in America, at Plymouth, Massachusetts. To provide wind bracing, this slender structure used a technique previously found only in bridge construction called arched portal bracing. Rounded corner window bays, like these on the Old Colony Building, were once common to many buildings in downtown Chicago. Now, because of the loss of many older downtown structures, the Old Colony Building remains as the sole Loop survivor with such windows. (ACB)

FISHER BUILDING [E]. Charles Atwood, of D.H. Burnham & Co., 1896; 343 S. Dearborn Street (**D4**). The Fisher Building, with its faceted surface of undulating windows, bears a strong resemblance to the Reliance Building, which was completed by D.H. Burnham & Co. just one year earlier (see p. 47). Like the Reliance, this building was erected quickly—the steel frame went up in only 25 days. Terra-cotta sea creatures ornament the lower floors, a reference to the developer, Lucius G. Fisher. This view, from the southeast, includes a corner of Old Colony Building in the left foreground and the Monadnock Building, between the Old Colony Building and the Fisher Building, behind. (R)

FISHER BUILDING, VIEWED FROM THE SOUTHWEST. The following, written by Carl Condit in *The Chicago School of Architecture,* aptly describes this image: "To appreciate the Fisher Building one has to see it in the late afternoon of a winter day. The fading daylight softens the redundant ornamental detail; the lighting within transforms the wall into a glittering and transparent sheath crossed by thin horizontal and vertical lines." A corner of the Old Colony Building is visible at right. (ACB)

FISHER BUILDING, WITH NORTHERN ADDITION. Addition: Peter J. Weber, of D.H. Burnham & Co., 1907. This later view shows the taller northern section, to the left of the earlier building. (v Enter the earlier building from Dearborn; at the left are original elevator gates. On the second floor, look for the original mosaic floor and marble walls, reminiscent of the Reliance Building.) (VOH)

MONADNOCK BUILDING [E]. Burnham & Root, 1889–91, Holabird & Roche, 1893; 53 W. Jackson Boulevard (**D5**). The Monadnock Building was constructed in two phases, by two different architectural firms. This view from Van Buren Street mainly shows the later, southern half, designed by Holabird & Roche, which used steel-frame construction and terra-cotta cladding. (CT)

MONADNOCK BUILDING, EAST FAÇADE.

The Monadnock Building. Chicago.

The earlier northern half, by Burnham & Root, is the architectural star of this building. It appears here, unfortunately not clearly, on the right. The construction is noteworthy. It is the heaviest and tallest wall-bearing structure in Chicago and was the last masonry skyscraper built. The structure's tremendous weight required walls six and a half feet thick at the street level. The resulting high material cost and very dark ground floor proved once and for all that metal-frame construction was the best solution for high-rise structures. The building is also significant because of its design. The developer's insistence on no exterior ornamentation, and Root's solution to that design constraint, produced a building of uncommon beauty which also predicted the direction of modern architecture. Designed for possible future division into four separate office buildings, it was originally planned to have four names—Monadnock, Kearsarge, Katahdin, and Wachusett. (v When the light is right, it's possible to make out the nearly-obliterated word "KEARSARGE" above the doorway of 314 S. Dearborn.) (C)

DEARBORN STREET, NORTH FROM VAN BUREN. The Monadnock Building is the building on the left, and the abrupt transition between the north and south sections can be seen. Note the flaring base of the north building, and its deep-set windows. Beyond, on the left, are the Federal Building and the Marquette Building. The vantage point for this view was probably the elevated train station, which crosses over Dearborn at Van Buren. (A)

DEARBORN STREET, NORTH FROM MONADNOCK BUILDING. Again, the distinctive base of the north half of the Monadnock Building can be seen at the immediate left. Across Jackson Boulevard, on the left, is the Federal Building and diagonally across the intersection, the Great Northern Hotel. In 1909, the sender wrote: "Dear Folks, We are all well & happy. So far the weather is beautiful and we are making hay while the sun shines. Katherine & I go trotting every day to see the parks and there is so much to see…" (DP-**1907**)

GREAT NORTHERN HOTEL [D], SOUTHWEST CORNER. Burnham & Root, 1892; 237 S. Dearborn Street (**D6**). This view depicts the Great Northern Hotel, which faced Dearborn Street. On the right, facing Jackson Boulevard is the attached and slightly taller Great Northern Office Building. (IW)

GREAT NORTHERN HOTEL, NORTHWEST CORNER. The design of the Great Northern Hotel was probably influenced by the Hyde Park Hotel, constructed five years earlier in Chicago's Hyde Park neighborhood. Approaching the project as they would an office building, Burnham & Root planned it with careful regard to space and light and used the most modern construction techniques available. This, combined with their sensitive treatment of the exterior, resulted in one of the finest achievements of the Chicago School. The building on the left, attached, is the Hotel Majestic. Message on back reads: "9/3. I saw Mr. Mueller a few minutes today. They are not quite ready for a deal." (FP)

GREAT NORTHERN HOTEL, INTERIOR VIEW OF CAFE. The Great Northern Hotel was demolished in 1940, and the site remained vacant for many years. The Dirksen Federal Building stands there today. Message: "July 8th. My dear Miss Perkins: We went fishing yesterday in Diamond Lake. No we didn't get any diamonds and very few fish. We are having a dandy vacation. Will tell you all about it when you come up. Yours J. P. M." (1913)

Hotel Majestic [D]. D.H. Burnham & Co., 1893; 29 West Quincy (**D7**). The façade of this building was designed to harmonize with the adjacent Great Northern Hotel, omitted in this depiction (see postcard at top of previous page). The pattern of windows, bays, and horizontal course lines were repeated on the newer building, including one between the 13th and 14th floors, which matched the line beneath the cornice of the shorter Great Northern Hotel. The Hotel Majestic was demolished in 1961. The domed building in the background is the Federal Building. Sender's message: "Dear Folks. I am leaving Chicago in about an hour. I went on a sight seeing trip today. I haven't a bit of desire for the City as yet. With Love, Willard." (CT-1929)

Federal Building and Post Office [D]. Henry Ives Cobb, 1905; block bounded by Dearborn, Jackson, Clark, and Adams Streets (**D8**). The federal government commissioned this building to provide a Midwest location for conducting its affairs. Henry Ives Cobb outdid himself in his effort to design a building of appropriate magnificence; the interior alone cost more than $2,000,000. This card's message, posted June 15, 1908, while Chicago hosted the Republican National Convention, reads: "Warm weather, but excitement makes delegates forget the heat. Cordially, Albert V." (DB-1908)

Series 1094 A.   Government Building & New Post Office, Chicago.   Davidson Broth

71

U.S. COURT HOUSE (FEDERAL BUILDING). This Court House witnessed many historic events, such as the sentencing of Al Capone for income tax evasion. Caption on back reads: "Located in the loop of Chicago, The Court House was once Chicago's Post Office. It now houses many government agencies in Chicago and is sometimes called the second U.S. Capitol." (CP)

AERIAL VIEW, LOOKING NORTHEAST OVER THE FEDERAL BUILDING. This postcard was published one year after the Great Northern Hotel was demolished. The Hotel Majestic (p. 71) now stands alone (note its exposed and blank west wall, in the lower right corner). Many other recognizable skyscrapers appear in the distance. From caption on back: "Soaring pinnacles and lofty towers—symbolic of the soaring ambitions and lofty ideals which make Chicago truly the City Beautiful." (CT-**1941**)

DOME OF THE FEDERAL BUILDING. An impressive 300-foot high octagonal dome surmounted Chicago's Federal Building. More than one hundred feet in diameter, it was larger than the dome of the U.S. Capitol Building, in Washington D.C. In 1965, Cobb's 1905 Federal Building was demolished to make way for a new Federal Center. The Kluczynski Federal Building, a U.S. Post Office, the Metcalfe Federal Building, and a plaza are now located on the site. (VOH)

MARQUETTE BUILDING [E]. Holabird & Roche, 1893–95; 140 S. Dearborn Street (**D9**). The Marquette Building was named to honor explorer and Jesuit priest, Jacques Marquette, who was the first European to describe the location that would become Chicago. One of the Chicago's most notable early skyscrapers, it is in the midst of a meticulous four-year restoration. Message, sent in 1905: "Nov. 11. I have 105 cards now. This is a beautiful bldg inside. Has painting on the walls & marble floors. Just an office bldg too." (v Don't miss the reliefs over the building's entrance and the mosaic murals inside, depicting scenes from Marquette's expedition.) (ECK-1905)

View South on Dearborn, from Monroe Street. All of the buildings shown here are gone. On the left side, the three nearest buildings from left to right are: the **Commercial National Bank [D]** (**D11**); **Adams Express Company [D]** (**D10**); and The Fair (see p. 57). On the right side, in the foreground, is the **First National Bank Building [D]** [Burling & Whitehouse, 1881; northwest corner of Dearborn and Monroe Streets (**D12**)]. The sender writes: "Leave for home Wed. Chi. just a little too small and slow for me." (ACB-1906)

DEARBORN ST. SOUTH OF MONROE STREET, CHICAGO, ILL. 1646

MADISON STREET, EAST FROM DEARBORN, CHICAGO

View East from Dearborn, at Madison Street. This view includes buildings on State Street and Michigan Avenue. From left to right are the Boston Store (p. 48), Mandel Brothers (and Annex) (pp. 49–50), Montgomery Ward Building (p. 32), and Carson Pirie Scott & Co. (p. 51). The entrance to the McVickers Theater appears on the right. (VOH)

MADISON STREET, CHICAGO, ILL.   C-13

VIEW EAST FROM DEARBORN, AT MADISON STREET. The large building on the right is the **Tribune Building [D]** [Holabird & Roche, 1902 (**D13**)], home of the Chicago Tribune until it outgrew the space and moved to the Tribune Tower (see p. 119). To the left of the Tribune Building is the **McVickers Theater [D]** [Adler & Sullivan, 1883; 25 W. Madison Street (**D14**)]. The first McVickers Theater was built here in 1857. It was destroyed in 1871 by the Chicago Fire and rebuilt in 1872; here Sarah Bernhardt made her Chicago debut. In 1885, the interior of the theater underwent a major renovation by Adler and Sullivan. Another fire damaged the building in 1890. Adler and Sullivan designed the reconstruction and added a floor of offices above; this postcard depicts the building in that configuration. Finally, in the early 1920s, the theater was torn down and a movie theater of the same name was built on the site. The tall white building behind is the Carson Pirie Scott store.

Madison St. looking East from Dearborn St., Tribune Bldg. at the Corner, McVickers Theatre next, Chicago.

A SLIGHTLY LATER VIEW EAST FROM DEARBORN, AT MADISON. Compare this to the card above. These views illustrate the architectural game of leap-frog taking place at this time. As construction techniques rapidly developed, each round of building seemed to produce structures double the height of the last. The Chicago Building (p. 52), constructed in 1904 to the east of the McVickers Theater, stands twice as tall as the McVickers, and the recently towering Carson Pirie Scott building is now dwarfed by the Heyworth Building (p. 37), erected to the east of it in 1905. (FP)

76

VIEW EAST ON WASHINGTON STREET FROM DEARBORN, WITH PORTLAND BLOCK. Moving north a block, this was the view looking east from Dearborn. The building at right was the **Portland Block [D]** [William Le Baron Jenney, 1872; southwest corner of Dearborn and Washington Streets (**D15**)], considered an important forerunner of the Chicago School commercial building. Constructed of masonry walls with some interior cast-iron columns, its exterior was plainly ornamented and faced with brick. This contrasted sharply with neighboring buildings, all heavily ornamented and of cut or planed stone. Appreciation of this building and its emphasis on practical matters—providing light, interior conveniences, and economy—began to drive the design process of other architects as well. It was demolished in 1933. The Reliance Building (p. 47) and Columbus Memorial Building (p. 46) appear in the center. (A)

UNITY BUILDING AND CHEMICAL BANK BUILDING. The tall building on the left is the **Unity Building [D]** [Clinton J. Warren, 1892; 127 N. Dearborn Street (**D17**)]. This 17-story building stood here until 1989 when it was demolished for the Block 37 project. (v A plaque in the sidewalk at the site of the building commemorates the upcoming centennial of the very first Rotary meeting, held in Room 711 of the Unity Building, in 1905.) To the right of the Unity Building is the **Chemical Bank Building [D]** [Burnham & Root, 1889; 115–121 N. Dearborn Street (**D16**)]. Developed as a speculative office building, the Chemical Bank Building was constructed of metal framing, quickly erected and, because of the somewhat confused façade ornamentation, is not considered one of Root's best works. (A)

VIEW EAST ON RANDOLPH STREET. The **Schiller Building (Garrick Theater) [D]** [Adler & Sullivan, 1892; 64 W. Randolph Street (**D18**)], was another highly successful theater-office structure by Alder & Sullivan. It succeeded both technically—the theater's acoustics and sightlines were nearly perfect—and aesthetically. In 1960, a strong and protracted effort was mounted to save the structure from demolition. Eventually, when funding to restore the building could not be secured, the building was razed. Adjacent, on the right, is the **Borden Block [D]** [Adler & Sullivan, 1880; northwest corner of Randolph and Dearborn Streets (**D19**)], which was the first building designed by the team of Adler & Sullivan. It was demolished in 1916 when Woods Theater was built. Further right is the **Delaware Building [E]** [Wheelock & Thomas, 1874; 36 W. Randolph Street (**D20**)]; it currently houses a fast-food restaurant on the ground floor. The Masonic Temple (p. 43) is visible in the distance. (v Enter the Delaware Building from Randolph Street to see the *c.* 1880s second-floor galleried light well.) (IW-1910)

VIEW WEST ON RANDOLPH STREET—WOODS THEATER AND SCHILLER BUILDING. In the foreground is **Woods Theater [D]**, [Marshall & Fox, 1917; northwest corner of Randolph and Dearborn Streets (**D19**)], which stood on the site of the Borden Block (see above). It was demolished in 1989. Caption on back reads: "This view represents one of the main theatrical sections of Chicago's Loop. The picture shows the Woods Bldg. housing the Woods Theatre, The Schiller Bldg., where the Garrick Theatre is located and the Ashland Block, containing the Olympic Theatre." (MRS-1922)

Five

CLARK STREET

Clark Street has functioned as a government center since 1835, when Chicago's first city hall was built on Clark Street between Randolph and Washington Streets. The current County Building and City Hall were erected here in 1907 and 1911. Neighboring office buildings like the demolished Ashland Block were largely occupied by lawyers. Not every building related to the city's government, as these postcards show. Also adjacent were the Chicago Opera House, Sherman House Hotel, and the Methodist church. Since 1845, the corner of Clark and Washington Streets has been the site of a Methodist church. The current building, the Chicago Temple, was erected in 1923 and holds a record variously described as the world's tallest church, world's tallest church-building, and world's tallest church spire.

BIRD'S-EYE VIEW, LOOKING NORTH FROM ADAMS STREET, C. 1893. This postcard, based on a photograph probably taken from the Home Insurance Building *c.* 1893, depicts buildings along La Salle and Clark Streets. Clark Street runs diagonally across the card from the lower right corner. The tall building straight ahead, on the left side, is the Tacoma Building (p. 103). Skyscrapers to the right of the Tacoma are the Chicago Opera House (p. 86), Ashland Block (p. 81), Schiller Building (p. 78), Unity Building (p. 77), and Masonic Temple (p. 43). (PS)

Clark Street

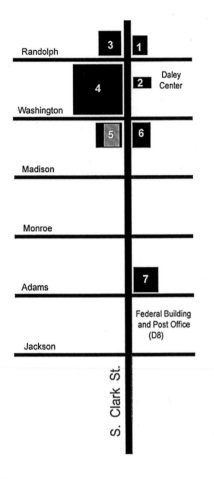

C1. Ashland Block
C2. City Hall Square Building
C3. Sherman House Hotel
C4. City Hall and County Building
C5. Chicago Opera House; Conway Building
C6. Chicago Temple Building
C7. Commercial National Bank Building

Ashland Block, Clark and Randolph Sts., Chicago.

ASHLAND BLOCK [D]. D.H. Burnham & Co., 1892; 155 N. Clark Street (**C1**). This office building was completed after Root's death, but the design shows his influence, resembling the earlier Great Northern Hotel in its appearance, materials, and construction. Because of the building's proximity to the City Hall and Court House, many tenants were lawyers, and the building contained a 7,000 volume law library for their convenience. The Ashland Block was demolished in 1949. The Schiller Building (p. 78) appears at right. (FP)

CITY HALL SQUARE BUILDING [D].
Christian A. Eckstorm, 1912; 139 N. Clark Street (**C2**). In this view, looking north on Clark Street, the neo-classical high-rise building on the right was City Hall Square Building. The 21-story office building faced City Hall, and its façade featured ornamental stone cladding on the uppermost and lowest floors. The building was demolished to make way for the Richard J. Daley Center, built in 1965. Visible in the distance, across Randolph Street, is the Ashland Block. (VOH)

SHERMAN HOUSE HOTEL [D]. Holabird & Roche, 1911; northwest corner of Clark and Randolph Streets (**C3**). The Sherman House Hotel was one of Chicago's longest-operating hotels. The first Sherman House was constructed on this site in 1845. The building depicted here, built in 1911, was the fourth and final Sherman House; it was enlarged in the 1920s and the green mansard roof shown here removed. During that period, the Sherman House's College Inn was a popular evening destination, and songs by resident bandleader Isham Jones and his unique style of dance music became known across the country. The building was demolished in 1983 to make way for the James R. Thompson Center, completed in 1985, which now stands on the site. (VOH)

STREET SCENE, LOOKING NORTH ON CLARK STREET FROM WASHINGTON STREET. The large looming building in this view is the County Building, constructed in 1907. Beyond it, on the left, is the third Sherman House Hotel. In the foreground, on the left, is a corner of the Chicago Opera House (see p. 86). (VOH)

CITY HALL AND COUNTY COURTHOUSE [D]. James J. Egan, 1885; block bounded by Randolph, Clark, Washington and La Salle Streets (**C4**). Begun soon after the Chicago Fire, this building took almost 12 years and more than $5 million to complete. Incredibly, it was demolished only 21 years later. Message reads: "Chicago Nov 12th 04. Dear Mamie, This is a 'Rush' corner, but it does not look it. Hereon Building is heavy stone—What is the 'columns' stand out heavy looking and 'tis a fine sight. Chicago is a grand place—but not to live in—for me. Chas." (ECK-1904)

NEW COUNTY BUILDING [E]. Holabird & Roche, 1907; 118 N. Clark Street (**C4**). The present City Hall and County Building, built on the site of the building shown above, is actually composed of two separate structures that were built at different times. The New County Building was constructed first and for several years stood beside the Old City Hall, visible to the left. Holabird & Roche's design, with its multi-story base and columns above, seems to have been influenced by the earlier building. (VOH)

MAIN CORRIDOR, NEW COUNTY BUILDING. The building's interior, noteworthy for its mosaics and vaulted ceilings, has remained mostly unchanged. The sender comments, "Isn't this lovely?" (VOH-1907)

COMPLETED CITY HALL (AND COUNTY BUILDING) [E]. Holabird & Roche, 1911; 121 N. La Salle Street (**C4**). This postcard depicts the building completed, with the new matching City Hall in place behind the County Building. During the construction of the New County Building and City Hall, offices moved temporarily to the Municipal Courts Building on Michigan Avenue (see p. 28). (v Images and descriptions of Chicago's earlier city halls are displayed in City Hall's second floor elevator lobby.) (VOH)

CHICAGO OPERA HOUSE [D]. Henry Ives Cobb & Charles S. Frost, 1885; southwest corner of Clark and Washington Streets (**C5**). Little is known about the structural support of the Chicago Opera House. The extent of glass, especially on the lower two floors, suggests metal

framing may have been used. Regardless, the character of this building's façade, with its shallow reveals and expanse of glass, was quite forward-thinking and the building is considered one of the most important erected in Chicago in the 1880s. It was demolished in 1912 when the Conway Building was erected here (next page). The tall building at right is the Chamber of Commerce Building (see p. 107). (R-1907)

CHICAGO OPERA HOUSE. This view more clearly shows the east elevation. (ECK-**1907**)

The Conway Building,
Chicago.

CONWAY BUILDING [E]. D.H. Burnham & Co. and Graham, Burnham & Co., 1913; 111 W. Washington Street (**C5**). Built on the former site of the Chicago Opera House, this building, now called the Chicago Title & Trust Building, was the last to come out of Daniel Burnham's office before his death. Its four rounded corners are a distinctive feature. On reverse is this message from sender: "Chicago, Ill. Aug 6 1916, Dear Friend, We are having warm weather in Chicago. Buying winter goods. With Kind Regards, Mrs. H. L." (MSR–1916)

248 THE CHICAGO TEMPLE BUILDING, BY NIGHT, CHICAGO

CHICAGO TEMPLE BUILDING [E]. Holabird & Roche, 1923; 77 W. Washington Street (**C6**). According to the *Guinness Book of World Records*, this is the world's tallest church. Because the building also contains offices, some prefer the title "world's tallest church-building." From 1924 to 1930, it was the tallest building in Chicago. Caption on back reads: "… surmounted by a 140 ft. tower, in early French Gothic architecture with Tubular chimes in the spire 500 feet above the street. A twelve foot cross is lighted by six tiers of floodlights every evening from sunset until midnight. …. Offices occupy the upper 19 stories." The building contains the street-level sanctuary and a small chapel in the spire, called the "Temple in the Sky." (v The church offers free guided tours daily.) (ACC)

COMMERCIAL NATIONAL BANK BUILDING [E]. D.H. Burnham & Co., 1907; 72 W. Adams Street (**C7**). The lobby of this building connects with the lobby of the Marquette Building (p. 74), visible to the right. The northwest corner of the old Federal Building (p. 71) appears in right foreground. This building now houses offices for the Chicago Public Schools. (v It was once known as the Edison Building; look above the entrances for remnants of that name.) (SHK)

COMMERCIAL NATIONAL BANK BLDG., CHICAGO, ILL.

Six

LA SALLE STREET

La Salle Street, the heart of Chicago's financial district, is sometimes called the Wall Street of Chicago. Located along its length are numerous trading, banking, and insurance concerns. The Chicago Board of Trade has operated at its southern end since 1885. Many of the city's most important early buildings such as the Home Insurance Building, Tacoma Building, and others included in this chapter, were constructed along La Salle Street. Ironically, the economic pressures that led to their original creation remain in effect and have also brought on their destruction. The 1972 razing of the Chicago Stock Exchange was one of Chicago's greatest architectural losses.

LA SALLE STREET, LOOKING NORTH FROM JACKSON BOULEVARD. This view, from the Chicago Board of Trade Building, shows that the canyon-like character of La Salle Street existed even at this early date (*c.* 1900). On the right is the Illinois Trust and Savings Bank, with the Rookery and Home Insurance Building beyond. (CT)

La Salle Street

L1. Chicago Board of Trade
L2. Phenix Building
L3. Insurance Exchange Building
L4. Illinois Trust & Savings Bank
L5. The Rookery
L6. Insurance Exchange
L7. Home Insurance Building; Field Building
L8. Marshall Field Wholesale Store
L9. Woman's Temple
L10. Northern Trust Co. Building
L11. Borland Building
L12. New York Life Building
L13. National Life Building
L14. Central YMCA (Association Bldg.)
L15. Otis Building
L16. Roanoke Tower
L17. Tacoma Building
L18. Hotel La Salle
L19. Chicago Stock Exchange
L20. Chicago Record Herald Building
L21. Chamber of Commerce Building;
Foreman National Bank Building
L22. Burnham Building

CHICAGO BOARD OF TRADE [D]. W.W. Boyington, 1885; 141 W. Jackson Boulevard (**L1**). The Chicago Board of Trade was formed in 1848 and operated in several locations until 1885, when this structure was erected. Within its walls was an enormous five-story high room used for buying and selling wheat and corn. A 300-foot high central tower was removed around 1895. This building was demolished in 1929, and the current Chicago Board of Trade building was built on the site. (FP-1913)

VIEW EAST ON JACKSON BOULEVARD, FROM THE BOARD OF TRADE. On the right, beyond the Board of Trade, is the **Phenix (Phoenix) Building [D]** [Burnham & Root, 1886, 1892; 111 W. Jackson Boulevard (**L2**)]. The two top floors shown here were added in 1892; before that addition, the building was very similar in appearance to The Rookery. The Phenix was also known as the Western Union Building and later, as the Austin Building. (With magnification one can read a sign on the corner of the building that says "Western Union Telegraphs.") The structure was demolished in 1959. The Monadnock Building (p. 67) is the tall building appearing in the distance, beyond the Phenix. (HCL)

91

INTERIOR, BOARD OF TRADE. "What makes the Board of Trade building notable is that it holds the Wheat Pit; which is not a sunken amphitheater . . . but a place far from sunken, reached by a stairway to the second floor. There one sees a big open hall, tall-windowed. One sees masses of excited men. One hears a roar of sound, a rumbling shouting, strident boom of human voices, rising and falling, sinking in volume only to break into greater and more vociferous noise. And, intermittently, when the tumult and the shouting dies, one hears the staccato ticking of the rows of telegraph instruments off at one side. At regular intervals stand four big platforms, each three steps up from the floor, and three are devoted to corn, to grain, to provisions, and the other is the so-called Wheat Pit. And what gigantic struggles have centered there!" (*The Book of Chicago*, 1920.) (KK-**1900**)

INSURANCE EXCHANGE BUILDING [E]. D.H. Burnham & Co., 1912; Graham, Anderson, Probst and White, 1928; 175 W. Jackson Boulevard (**L3**). This building was constructed in two sections, and the northern half shown here was completed first, in 1912. At one time more insurance companies were headquartered here than in any other building in the world. The exterior is faced with enameled bricks and has terra-cotta ornamentation. A corner of the Board of Trade appears at left. (v The interior has been modernized. Walk through the lobby to see the central light well, now capped with a skylight.) (VOH-1914)

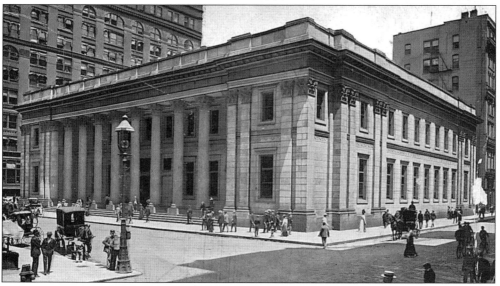

ILLINOIS TRUST AND SAVINGS BANK [D]. D.H. Burnham & Co., 1897; Jackson and La Salle Streets (**L4**). Two significant events occurred between the construction of The Rookery at left (also by Daniel Burnham) and the construction of this structure that help explain the difference in their styles. The first was the death of Burnham's partner John Root, who, of the two, was perhaps the more versed in the Chicago idiom expressed in The Rookery. The second event was the World's Columbian Exposition and the subsequent popularity of classical designs that resulted from it. This bank was demolished in 1924 to build the Illinois Merchants Bank. (AHC)

THE ROOKERY [E]. Burnham & Root, 1885–88; 209 S. La Salle Street (**L5**). The 11-story Rookery was once the tallest structure in Chicago. The exterior of red granite, pressed brick, and terra-cotta presents a dazzling display of ornamentation. The interior is equally impressive. The light court retains changes made by Frank Lloyd Wright in a 1905 remodeling. The entire structure was magnificently restored in the early 1990s. (v Look to your left as you enter the skylit central court. An area of flooring, edged with metal, is the original mosaic floor (the rest is a reproduction.) Also, look on the back of the nearby column to see the appearance of the columns before Wright's marble redo.) (EP-**1907**)

VIEW NORTH ON LA SALLE, FROM QUINCY STREET. The base of The Rookery appears at right. Beyond The Rookery, on the right, are the Home Insurance Building (next image) and Borland Building (p. 99). The **Insurance Exchange [D]** [Burnham & Root, 1884–85 (**L6**)], on the left, was demolished in 1912. Beyond is the curved corner of the Woman's Temple (p. 98). Message on back reads: "My Dear Mrs T—Am I going to be made happy by having you here next week—Let me know, Mary." (1910)

Home Insurance Bldg.,
Chicago.

HOME INSURANCE BUILDING [D]. William Le Baron Jenney, 1884–85; northeast corner of La Salle and Adams Streets (**L7**). Considered by many to be the first skyscraper, this building made the first extensive use of iron and steel framing, which allowed the structure to rise to nine stories. (Additional floors, depicted here, were added later.) Because the exterior walls no longer provided support, Jenney was able to increase the size of the window openings. Concerned that a building of so many stories would present a monotonous appearance, Jenney interrupted the elevations with ornament. (Burnham & Root did the same with The Rookery.) The Home Insurance Building was an immediate sensation, and continued to draw sightseers for many years: "… No longer a skyscraper in the modern acceptance of the term, this structure still is of sufficient altitude to attract attention. It possesses unusual interest to the sightseer in that it is a monument to the genius of the late W.L.B. Jenney in whose brain modern steel construction was first conceived." (*A Guide to the City of Chicago,* 1909.) (IW-1910)

150—Field Building, Chicago

FIELD BUILDING [E]. Graham, Anderson, Probst & White, 1934; 135 S. La Salle Street (**L7**). The Home Insurance Building was demolished in 1931 and the Field Building, later known as the La Salle Bank Building, was constructed on the site. This was one of the last large buildings to be erected in Chicago before the construction hiatus brought on by the Great Depression and World War II. From the caption on back: "... Chicago's largest and one of its most excellent office buildings, rising to a height of 530 feet above the street. The building is strikingly impressive by its very simplicity of architecture. Owned and operated by the Estate of Marshall Field." (v Don't miss the beautiful Art Deco lobby.) (CT-**1941**)

CHICAGO BOARD OF TRADE [E]. Holabird & Root, 1930; 141 W. Jackson Boulevard (**L1**). The 1930 Chicago Board of Trade Building, an Art Deco masterpiece, creates a dramatic focal point to the southern end of La Salle Street. Because the Illinois Merchants Bank Building and Federal Reserve Bank, on the left and right, were constructed six and eight years before the new Board of Trade, the old Board of Trade Building (p. 91) no longer matched the scale of the street. Also, its style had fallen out of favor: "... The Board of Trade building ... is not in keeping with the wealth and dignity of the banking and commercial buildings. It is ornate and unbeautiful, of a mixed style of architecture, with two tall stone women over the entrance and with a sort of pointed effect from some little towers that barely rise higher than the roof.... [A] new building is expected to be built." (*The Book of Chicago*, 1920.) Note The Rookery, at near left. (CT-**1941**)

146—Looking Down La Salle Street, Chicago, Chicago Board of Trade in Background

MARSHALL FIELD WHOLESALE STORE [D]. Henry Hobson Richardson, 1887; block bounded by Adams, Wells, Quincy, and Franklin Streets (**L8**). This building profoundly influenced American architecture. This structure (and other Richardson buildings) contributed to the popularity of the Romanesque-Revival style in the 1880–1890s. The Chicago School, and Louis Sullivan in particular, were affected by it, as seen in the Auditorium Building (p. 17). Richardson died at the age of 47; this was one of his final designs. (1907)

MARSHALL FIELD WHOLESALE STORE. Regarding its demolition in 1930 to build a parking lot, H.R. Hitchcock observed that, "It was really sacrificed to the urban congestion the skyscraper had created. . . . [T]his building should have been preserved and all the blocks around torn down to display one of the greatest monuments of architecture in America." Today the building's exact footprint is occupied by a parking structure beside the Sears Tower. It's interesting to imagine the Marshall Field Wholesale Store not having been demolished and standing at the foot of the Sears Tower! (VOH)

Chicago. Woman's Temple.

WOMAN'S TEMPLE [D]. Burnham & Root, 1892; 102–116 S. La Salle Street (**L9**). This building was designed for Frances Willard and the Women's Christian Temperance Union. Burnham & Root struggled with the design, attempting to create a building that was feminine, spiritually uplifting, and also (another request of the clients) "able to generate large revenue." It seems they succeeded. In the years immediately after Root's death, the Woman's Temple was Burnham & Root's most admired building. It was demolished in 1926. (AMW-1910)

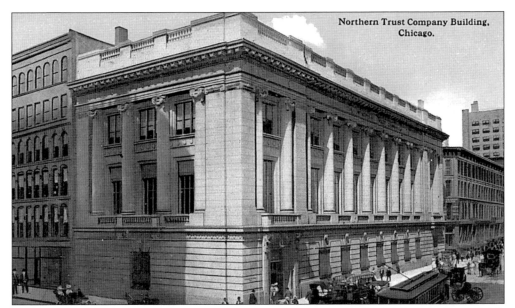

Northern Trust Company Building, Chicago.

NORTHERN TRUST COMPANY BUILDING [E]. Frost & Granger, 1905; 50 S. La Salle Street (**L10**). In 1928, this building received a two-story addition but otherwise has remained mostly unchanged from its appearance in this *c.* 1905 view. Caption on back reads: "This is probably one of the most artistic banking structures in the country. The Northern Trust Co. are the sole occupants of the building, which is situated on the Northwest corner of La Salle and Monroe Streets." (EA)

BORLAND BUILDING [D]. Shepley, Rutan & Coolidge, 1906; 105 S. La Salle Street (**L11**). The façade of this building, of Bedford limestone and Roman brick, was heavily ornamented at base and cornice. In the left foreground is the New York Life Building. Beyond the Borland are the Home Insurance Building and the Rookery. This photograph was taken from the roof of the Northern Trust Company Building (note cornice edge at right); a sliver of the Woman's Temple appears along right edge. (ACD)

NEW YORK LIFE BUILDING [E]. Jenney & Mundie, 1894; 39 S. La Salle Street (**L12**). This building is one of three, all in a row and all still standing, designed by Jenney & Mundie. It is said to be the first steel-frame building that was built not from the ground up, but with several floors constructed simultaneously. It was later known as the La Salle–Monroe Building. (v The original lobby remains. Note the marble stairs, walls and ceilings, and vintage light fixtures including a *c.* 1930s chandelier.) (KK)

NATIONAL LIFE BUILDING [E]. Jenney & Mundie, 1902; Holabird & Root, 1940; 29 S. La Salle Street (**L13**). This building appears modern today because it was re-clad in 1940 and the neo-classical façade, shown here, removed. Other names for the building have been the Equitable Building and Barrister Hall. On the right is the New York Life Building. (v Proceed through the modernized lobby to the original hallway beyond. Note marble walls and ceiling, old shop doors, etc. Turn left at the end and exit through door to alley-like street called Arcade Place. Here the building's original exterior can be seen—note enameled brick and old storefront windows along Arcade Place.) (BS-1907)

CENTRAL YMCA (ASSOCIATION BUILDING)
[E]. Jenney & Mundie, 1893; 19 S. La Salle
Street (**L14**). This building was constructed
shortly before the panic and depression of
1893. Not obvious from the street, the building
is actually L-shaped with a narrow façade on
La Salle Street and an expansive façade along
Arcade Place to the south. The National Life
Building can be seen on the right. Message
from sender: "Dear Helen: —Rec'd your photo
O.K. and want to thank you, ever & ever so
much for it. It certainly is grand. Is that your
chum? Will write soon. Ella." (WGM-1908)

YMCA BUILDING, FROM SOUTH. This view
depicts the south façade of the YMCA Building
and Arcade Place. The horizontal banding near
the top of the building was characteristic of
Jenney's work during this period. The peaked
roof that appears here has been replaced by a
three-story addition. (CT-1906)

Otis Building, Chicago.

OTIS BUILDING [E, EXTERIOR WALLS OF BASE ONLY]. Holabird & Roche, 1912; 10 S. La Salle Street (**L15**). When the Chemical Plaza Building was constructed on this site in 1989, the exterior walls of the Otis Building base were saved and incorporated into the base of the new office tower. Visible to the left is the Northern Trust Savings Bank and Woman's Temple. From caption on back: "This building is one of Chicago's latest skyscrapers, being 16 stories high, and ... is considered by architects to be one of the finest office buildings in the world as the entrance and all the corridors are lined with imported Italian statuary marble." (EA)

CHICAGO CENTRAL AERIAL BEACON AND ROANOKE TOWER [E]. Holabird & Roche, 1915, 1922, 1926; 11 S. La Salle Street (**L16**). Originally 16 stories tall, this building has been added to and renovated in subsequent years, most recently in 1984. This postcard depicts the structure following the 1926 tower addition; the view is looking west on Madison Street, across La Salle. Caption on back describes the tower's beacon: "The Central Chicago Aerial Beacon atop the Roanoke Tower . . . rises 45 feet from the roof of the tower to an elevation of 520 feet above the sidewalk, and contains 24 Neon light tubes in addition to two rotating beacon searchlights, each of 8,000,000 beam candle power. It is visible for a distance of 100 miles." (MRS-**1933**)

5420. TACOMA BLDG., CHICAGO.

TACOMA BUILDING [D]. Holabird & Roche, 1889; northeast corner of La Salle and Madison Streets (**L17**). Construction of the Tacoma Building involved many technical breakthroughs, including a new method of foundation construction and the first use of riveting in the erection of a metal skeletal frame (in this case, of wrought iron, cast iron and steel). The unusual projecting window bays were designed to increase light and air to the interior, to break up and reduce wind force, and finally, to create a sense of lightness and bring interest to the surface of the building. The Tacoma Building was demolished in 1929. The card's message, sent to Tacoma, Washington, in 1908, reads: "Mamma and I went down town this afternoon. Went through the Boston store. We found our way back easily and didn't get lost. We are staying at the Sherman House. Flossie." (EP-**1907**)

HOTEL LA SALLE [D]. Holabird & Roche, 1909; northwest corner of La Salle and Madison Streets (**L18**). The Hotel La Salle was an elegant hotel adjacent to the Chicago Stock Exchange. Its magnificent spaces, such as the walnut-paneled lobby, Louis XIV-style dining room, lavish ballroom and Rookwood Room (also called the Palm Room), made it one of the premier hotels in the city. The building was demolished in 1976 and its foundation reused for the construction of 2 N. La Salle Street, the building now on the site. (VOH-**1910**)

BLUE FOUNTAIN ROOM, HOTEL LA SALLE. This wood-paneled dining room, one of several in the La Salle Hotel, at one time featured the "Tango-Banjo Orchestra" and was fashionable with the after-theater crowd. Message from sender: "Chicago, Ill., 9-16-15. Am still on the go and take it from me it is surely hot here. Expect to go farther north Saturday & hope I find cooler weather there. Yours, W.M.R." (VOH-1915)

Chicago Stock Exchange [D]. Adler & Sullivan, 1894; 30 N. La Salle Street (**L19**). A masterpiece of Chicago architecture and one of Adler and Sullivan's finest works, this building was unfortunately demolished in 1972. The building's fine ironwork, especially of its elevator grills, and the ornate stenciling in the trading room were particularly noteworthy. The efforts to prevent the demolition of this building, and also of Adler & Sullivan's Schiller Building, gave rise to the preservation movement in Chicago. Salvaged elements of the building, including the entrance arch visible here, are now found in the collection of the Art Institute of Chicago, and elsewhere. Note the Chicago Record Herald Building, at right (see next). (ACB)

CHICAGO RECORD HERALD BUILDING [D]. Burnham & Root, 1891; 161–65 W. Washington Street (**L20**). This picturesque building was described as being Romanesque below and Flemish above. Root's basic organization of the façade into three bays was similar to his Chicago Club (p. 19), built four years earlier. A bronze sculpture of a herald stood at the gable, and terra-cotta reliefs below also ornamented the façade. The newspaper's offices and press room, visible from a gallery, were on the first floor. The building, also known as the Herald Building and Andrews Building, was demolished in 1936. (KK-1905)

CHAMBER OF COMMERCE BUILDING [D].
Baumann & Huehl, 1889; southeast corner
of La Salle and Washington Streets (**L21**).
This building was another proto-skyscraper,
and it took the ideas of the Home
Insurance Building (p. 95) one step farther.
The building was almost fully framed of
bolted iron and steel. The base was less
massive than those of earlier buildings, even
the Home Insurance, and contained large
areas of glass. The full 13-story interior light
well was also significant. It was enclosed
at the top with a glass skylight and ornate
ironwork decorated the staircase railings
and cantilevered balconies. The building was
demolished in 1928. Note old City Hall, at
left. (MN-1906)

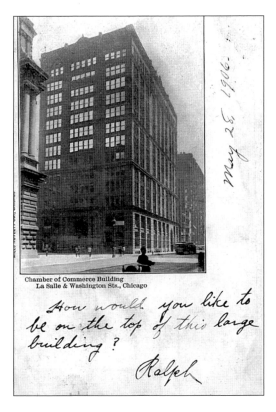

Chamber of Commerce Building
La Salle & Washington Sts., Chicago

How would you like to be on the top of this large building?

Ralph

FOREMAN NATIONAL BANK BUILDING [E].
Graham, Anderson, Probst & White, 1930; 33
N. La Salle Street (**L21**). The Foreman Building
was built on the site of Chamber of Commerce
(previous card). It has lost its original Art Deco
interior, but the exterior remains intact and is
a fine example of a 1930s-era skyscraper. The
Conway Building (p. 87) can be seen behind, on
the left. (MRS-**1933**)

BURNHAM BUILDING [E]. Burnham Bros., 1924; 160 N. La Salle Street (**L22**). This building, facing La Salle Street and opposite the Thompson Center, received a major remodeling in 1992 which changed the appearance of the façade significantly. A floor was added at the top and the open light well, created by the building's U shape, was enclosed by a glass curtain wall and skylight cap. (MRS)

LOOKING EAST ON RANDOLPH STREET, FROM LA SALLE STREET. On the right is the old City Hall and Courthouse. Major buildings on the left, from left to right, are The Sherman House, Ashland Block, Schiller Building, Borden Block, Delaware Building, and Masonic Temple. (ECK)

Seven

ALONG THE RIVER AND NORTH MICHIGAN AVENUE

In 1920, the aging and crowded Rush Street Bridge was replaced by a magnificent new river crossing at Michigan Avenue. The construction of the Michigan Avenue Bridge, and transformation of a narrow north side street called Pine Street into North Michigan Avenue, set the stage for development of the "Magnificent Mile." In 1926, on the south bank of the river, work began on remaking South Water Street into the world's first two-level street, Wacker Drive. The 1920s was a period of great growth and also a time of great development of the skyscraper form. The skyscrapers included here, built along the Chicago River and the Magnificent Mile, date from this period.

507:—NEWS AND CIVIC OPERA BUILDINGS. CHICAGO. ILL.

DAILY NEWS AND CIVIC OPERA BUILDINGS. These two buildings were both constructed on the eve of the Great Depression. Looking like a pair of armchairs, they face each other across the Chicago River. (GB)

Along the River & N. Michigan Ave.

R1. Chicago Civic Opera Building
R2. Daily News Building (Riverside Plaza)
R3. Engineering Building
R4. Builders Building
R5. Merchandise Mart
R6. Pure Oil Building
R7. Mather Tower
R8. London Guarantee & Accident Co.
R9. 333 Building
R10. Bell Building (Old Republic Building)
R11. Carbide & Carbon Building
R12. Wrigley Buildings
R13. Tribune Tower
R14. WGN Studio Building
R15. Medinah Athletic Club
       (Hotel Inter-Continental)
R16. Allerton Hotel
R17. American Furniture Mart (Lake Shore Place)
R18. Chicago Water Tower
R19. Palmolive Building
R20. Drake Hotel
R21. Drake Tower

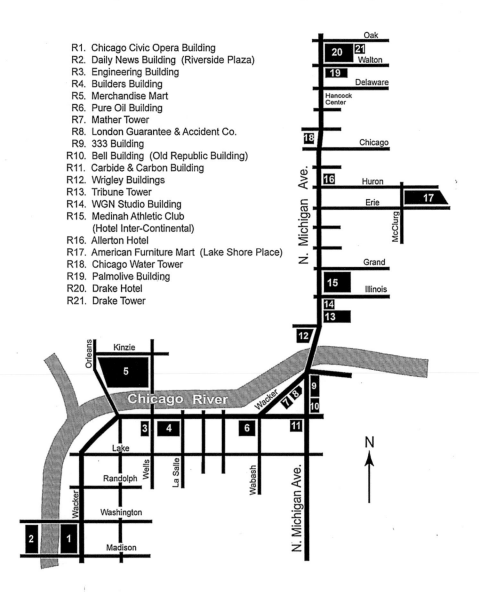

CHICAGO CIVIC OPERA BUILDING [E].
Graham, Anderson, Probst & White, 1929; 20 N.
Wacker Drive (**R1**). An office building wrapped
around two theaters, this structure was the last
real estate venture financed by electric railroad
and utilities tycoon Samuel Insull. Because
of the building's shape and the developer's
prominence, it was nicknamed "Insull's
Throne." The Civic Opera's grand opening
here, a performance of *Aida*, took place only
six days after the Stock Market crash of 1929.
The construction of this building led to the
closing of the Auditorium Theater, and Insull's
bankruptcy as well. (CT-**1941**)

171—Chicago Civic Opera Building,
Chicago

DAILY NEWS BUILDING [E]. Holabird & Root, 1929; 2 N. Riverside Plaza (**R2**). This building,
now called Riverside Plaza, was the first in Chicago built over railroad tracks using air rights.
It also was the first to incorporate a public plaza in the design. Caption: "At Madison, Canal,
Washington, and the river twenty-five stories in height, houses the plant and all editorial and
business departments of *The Daily News*, the studios of WMAQ, and other tenants."(MRS-**1933**)

"SKY-SCRAPER DISTRICT OF CHICAGO." This triple postcard was published in 1904 and views Chicago from the west side. The Chicago River can be seen along the card's left edge, Lake Michigan appears at the top, and the South Fork of the Chicago River crosses the view diagonally to the upper right. During this period, the buildings along the Chicago River were largely warehouses and factories. Closer to the river's mouth at Lake Michigan were riverside docks for passenger ship lines. An interesting aspect of this picture is the density of Chicago's downtown;

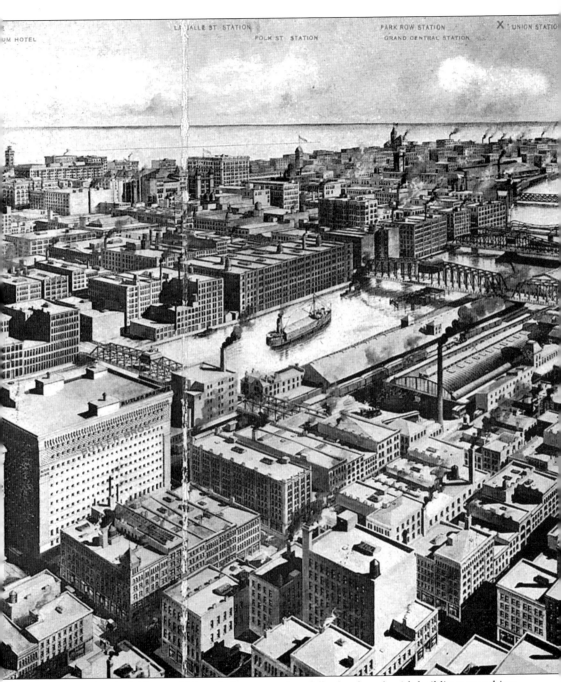

from early in the city's history, Chicago's downtown lots fully developed, with buildings stretching from lot line to lot line. Looking closely, the following are some of the buildings that can be found in this view: The Masonic Temple, Schiller Building, Ashland Block, Marshall Field's store, Reliance Building, Old City Hall and Courthouse, Chamber of Commerce Building, Chicago Opera House, Central YMCA, Woman's Temple, Home Insurance Building, The Rookery, Federal Building, Auditorium Building, and Illinois Central Depot. (ECK-**1904**)

VIEW SOUTHEAST ALONG THE CHICAGO RIVER, FROM THE MERCHANDISE MART. Taken from the Merchandise Mart, this view of the Chicago River looks east and shows buildings along Wacker Drive, including the Engineering Building and Builders Building (see below). (CLC-1943)

ENGINEERING BUILDING, CHICAGO, ILL.

ENGINEERING BUILDING [E]. Burnham Bros., 1928; 205 W. Wacker Drive (**R3**). This view of the Engineering Building is from the northeast, looking across the Chicago River. Note the elevated train tracks of the Well Street Bridge, in the foreground. The building's original entrance was off Wells Street; a 1982 renovation moved it to Wacker Drive. (v Bronze plaques in the lobby, originally from the elevator doors, depict gears and other engineering-related motifs.)

BUILDERS BUILDING [E]. Graham, Anderson, Probst & White, 1927; 222 N. La Salle Street (**R4**). The building trades developed this building and showcased their products in its four-story galleried atrium. The building was expanded in 1986 with a harmonious addition to the west and a four-story penthouse capping it all. Caption on back: "The Builders' Building is located at the intersection of Chicago's newest boulevard, Wacker Drive and La Salle St. It covers an area of 30,500 square feet and rises to the majestic height of 23 stories. An impressive feature of the Builders' Building is its vast marble rotunda." (v Visit the galleried atrium, still located in the center of the original building.) (MRS-1928)

115—The Merchandise Mart by Night, Chicago

MERCHANDISE MART [E]. Graham, Anderson, Probst & White, 1930; north bank of the Chicago River between Wells and Orleans Streets (**R5**). When first constructed, this was the world's largest building and, with 4.1 million square feet of rentable space and its own zip code, it still retains the title of world's largest commercial building (second only to the Pentagon in square footage). Built as a wholesale center for Marshall Field's & Co. stores, it now serves as a wholesale buying center, office building, and retail mall. (CT-**1941**)

In the panoramic image the following buildings are labeled: TRIBUNE TOWER, WRIGLEY BLDG., LONDON GUARANTEE & ACCIDENT BLDG., 333 BLDG., MATHER TOWER, BELL BLDG., PURE OIL BLDG.

VIEW EAST ON THE CHICAGO RIVER. This panoramic view includes many landmark skyscrapers erected during the 1920s. The **Bell Building [E]**, also called the Old Republic Building, [Vitzthum & Burns, 1925; 307 N. Michigan Avenue (**R10**)], was the first skyscraper constructed east of Michigan Avenue between the Chicago River and Grant Park, and enjoyed high visibility. The **Mather Tower [E]** [Herbert Hugh Riddle, 1928; 75 E. Wacker Drive (**R7**)], also called the Lincoln Tower, is Chicago's most slender skyscraper and was fifth tallest in the city when first built. (MRS-1932)

PURE OIL BUILDING [E]. Giaver and Dinkelberg; Thielbar and Fugard, associate architects, 1926; 35 E. Wacker Drive (**R6**). When first built, this was called the Jewelers Building and was the tallest building west of New York City. An unusual security feature was the 22-story parking garage in the center of the building; elevators brought jewelers' cars and delivery vehicles from Wacker Drive directly to the desired floor. The garage was converted to office space in 1940. During Prohibition, the belvedere at the top held a speakeasy. (v Note the "JB," for Jewelers Building, above the entrance and on metalwork within.) (MRS)

LONDON GUARANTEE AND ACCIDENT COMPANY BUILDING [E]. Alfred S. Alschuler, 1923; 360 N. Michigan Avenue (**R8**). This neo-classical-style building was constructed on what was once the site of the blockhouse of Fort Dearborn, the first permanent settlement in Chicago. A bronze relief above the entrance depicts the fort and its surroundings. The curve in the Chicago River here dictated the structure's unusual trapezoidal shape. The building has also been known as the Stone Container Building and Crain Communications Building. An award-winning historic renovation was recently completed. (v The ceiling of the entrance lobby is dazzling. Also spectacular is the view outside, looking north from the entrance at the Michigan Avenue Bridge and buildings across the Chicago River.) (UN)

VIEW OF THE PURE OIL BUILDING, LOOKING SOUTHEAST FROM ACROSS THE CHICAGO RIVER. The tallest building to the right of the Pure Oil Building is the Pittsfield Building (p. 40). Blocking the Pittsfield Building somewhat is the Masonic Temple (p. 43), captured here in one of the final years of its existence. To the left of the Pure Oil Building is the **Carbide and Carbon Building [E]** [Burnham Bros., 1929; 230 N. Michigan Avenue (**R11**)], recently remodeled into the Hard Rock Hotel. (GB)

SOUTH AND NORTH SECTIONS, BY NIGHT, CHICAGO   3A-H773

WRIGLEY BUILDINGS [E]. Graham, Anderson, Probst & White, 1919–24; 400 and 410 N. Michigan Avenue (**R12**). The Wrigley Building is, in fact, two buildings. The original south section features a tall clock tower patterned after a cathedral in Seville, Spain. The larger but less noticed north annex is connected by a breezeway at the street level, a third floor walkway, and a bridge at the 14th floor. The complex was built by the Wrigley Chewing Gum Company and still houses its corporate offices. The building is illuminated at night by intense floodlights. The reflective terra-cotta cladding is actually six shades of white, applied so that the building is increasingly whiter as it rises. Message, sent June 13, 1934, reads: "Dear friends: Just a line to let you know I am having a wonderful time, and a very busy one. Everything is going fine. Shall tell you all later. Mamma is all pepped up, having a grand time. Lovingly—Bessie." (MRS-1934)

MICHIGAN AVE. LOOKING NORTH
Showing Wrigley Building, Tribune and Medinah A.C.
CHICAGO

VIEW NORTH ON MICHIGAN AVENUE, WITH WRIGLEY BUILDING AND TRIBUNE TOWER. The Wrigley Building and Tribune Tower, to the left and right here, form a gateway to Michigan Avenue north of the Chicago River, known as the "Magnificent Mile." Shown here, on the east side of Michigan Avenue beyond the Tribune Tower, are the Medinah Athletic Club, Allerton Hotel, and Palmolive Building. The Water Tower appears straight ahead. (Note Michigan Avenue has not yet been realigned.) In the right foreground is the Tribune Tower's early smelly neighbor—the American Family Soap Factory. This photograph was probably taken from the 333 Building. (PPS-1933)

TRIBUNE TOWER [E]. Howells & Hood, 1923-25; 435 N. Michigan Avenue (**R13**). In 1922, on the occasion of the company's 75th anniversary, the Chicago Tribune sponsored an architectural competition for the design of a new headquarters to replace their offices on Dearborn Street (see p. 76). Seeking plans for "the most beautiful office building in the world," the Tribune offered $100,000 in prize money and received 263 entries. First prize was awarded to John Mead Howells and Raymond M. Hood for their Gothic skyscraper design. The contest and a traveling exhibit of the competition drawings generated much interest in the architectural community. Many believed Eliel Saarinen's second-prize entry (see also below) was superior. Louis Sullivan characterized the winning design as "evolved of dying ideas." The building's exterior features carvings and stone fragments from historic sites. (v The stone screen above the main entrance depicts characters from Aesop's fables. At the upper left and right are a howling dog and Robin Hood—visual puns of the architects' names. Pamphlets describing the building are available in the lobby.) (CT)

118—The Tribune Tower, Chicago

VIEW SOUTH FROM TRIBUNE TOWER. Still one of the city's most breathtaking views, this postcard depicts the impressive display of skyscrapers constructed here in the 1920s. From left to right: Bell Building, 333 Building, Carbide and Carbon Building, London Guarantee & Accident Company, Mather Tower, Pure Oil Building, and Wrigley Building. The design of the **333 Building** [E], [Holabird & Root, 1928; 333 N. Michigan Avenue (**R9**)], took inspiration from Eliel Saarinen's second-prize winning entry in the Tribune Tower contest. (GB-1943)

WGN RADIO BUILDING [E]. Howells & Hood, 1935; 441–445 N. Michigan Avenue (**R14**). Constructed just to the north of the Tribune Tower and of a matching Neo-Gothic design, this low limestone-clad building housed studios and offices for the Tribune Company's radio station.

155—Michigan Avenue, Looking North
Sheraton Hotel in Foreground
Chicago

Across the north and west façades of the building were carved the radio station's call letters "W G N," taken from the newspaper's masthead, "The World's Greatest Newspaper." The letters were removed from the building in 1961. Today, a retail store occupies the street-level space. (CT-**1941**)

VIEW NORTH ON MICHIGAN AVENUE, FROM WRIGLEY BUILDING. A corner of the Wrigley Building appears in the left foreground. Other buildings, from left to right, are the Allerton Hotel, Medinah Athletic Club, WGN Radio Building, and Tribune Tower. (CT-**1950**)

MEDINAH ATHLETIC CLUB [E]. Walter W. Ahlschlager, 1929; 505 N. Michigan Avenue (**R15**). Beginning in 1988, this building underwent a massive restoration. A quarter-of-a-billion dollars later, it reopened as the Hotel Inter-Continental. Originally a men's hotel for members of the Shrine organization called the Medinah Athletic Club, it was designed in a Romantic style with Neo-Egyptian, Spanish, and Near-Eastern elements. The hotel quickly foundered and ownership changed. From caption: "America's Finest Club . . . Constructed at a cost of nine million dollars, athletic facilities include two luxurious swimming pools, rifle range, gymnasium, bowling alleys, billiard rooms, handball courts and extensive health equipment. Residential facilities include 500 beautiful rooms, available to men, women and families. There are no affiliations necessary for membership." (v If possible, take the self-guided audio tour available at the front desk. It describes the restoration process and guides you through lobbies, ballrooms, and the historic swimming pool above the seventh floor ballroom. At the very least, be sure to see the original Tower Lobby, south of the new entrance.)

ALLERTON HOTEL [E]. Murgatroyd & Ogden, 1924; 140 E. Huron Street (**R16**). This was one of a chain of Allerton Hotels built in the 1920s that originally catered to single professional men, providing residential and traveler accommodations. The building was one of the first skyscrapers on North Michigan Avenue and its northern Italian Renaissance design incorporated roof setbacks as required by the 1923 zoning law; the first in Chicago to do so. The building had an 18-hole golf course in the basement and a ballroom at the top. In the 1940s, the Tip Top Tap, a cocktail lounge on the 23rd floor, replaced clubrooms and was opened to the public. Although the lounge closed in the 1960s, the historic sign has remained. (v The building has recently been renovated. Photographs of the original lobby hang inside the Huron Street entrance.) (FH-**1925**)

ALLERTON HOTEL

LEGEND:
— Blue Line: MICHIGAN AVENUE   4 SEVEN MINUTES TO LOOP
— Red Line: OUTER DRIVE   5 PALMOLIVE BUILDING
1 LAKE MICHIGAN   6 FURNITURE MART
2 OAK ST. BATHING BEACH   7 NORTHWESTERN UNIVERSITY
3 LINCOLN PARK AND ZOO   CHICAGO CAMPUS

Aerial View Showing Ideal Location of ALLERTON HOTEL — 701 N. MICHIGAN AVE. — CHICAGO 11, ILL.

AERIAL VIEW OF ALLERTON HOTEL AND SURROUNDINGS. This map locates neighboring landmarks such as Northwestern University, the Furniture Mart, and Lincoln Park. Message from sender: "Hi kids, I'm in Chic. since last Friday. I'm having a grand time. I'm in this hotel. Our room is on the 22nd floor. I've been swimming in Lake Michigan. Have gone to several museums. Was to Chinatown today. Very interesting. Love Alice." (CT-**1939**)

AMERICAN FURNITURE MART [E]. Henry Raeder Assocs., 1924 and George C. Nimmons & N. Max Dunning, 1926; 680 N. Lake Shore Drive (**R17**). Built to serve the wholesale furniture industry once centered in Chicago, the earlier eastern half is constructed of reinforced concrete. The western half is a steel-framed skyscraper and its blue-roofed tower was inspired by the Houses of Parliament. The Furniture Mart closed in 1979 and reopened in 1983 as residences and offices. (v Terra-cotta reliefs above the east entrance depict furniture making.) (CT-**1937**)

PALMOLIVE BUILDING [E]. Holabird & Root, 1929; 919 N. Michigan Avenue (**R19**). Currently being converted to condominiums, this former office building epitomizes the Art Deco style of skyscrapers with its strong vertical lines, roofline setbacks, and stylized ornamentation. Dramatic nighttime illumination highlights the building's sculptural qualities. The card's caption describes the powerful beacon at the top: "A spectacular night-time feature of the new Palmolive building is the Lindbergh Beacon. Mounted atop a shining bronze column, 603 feet above Chicago, its two billion candlepower beam is visible to aviators in the air as far east as Cleveland, Ohio, and as far south as St. Louis, Missouri." Message from sender, attending Century of Progress Exposition: "Arrived safe and the weather is just nice. Hope it will be nice tomorrow. Most are going to the fair tomorrow. Sincerely, Mrs. T." (CT-**1933**)

CHICAGO WATER TOWER AND PALMOLIVE BUILDING. The Palmolive Building and Drake Tower appear in the center distance. In the foreground are the **Chicago Water Tower and Pumping Station [E]**, [W.W. Boyington, 1866, 1869; 806 and 811 N. Michigan Avenue (**R18**)], among the few structures to survive the Chicago Fire of 1871. The Water Tower was built to conceal a 138-foot standpipe, since removed; the Pumping Station still operates. The buildings' style is called "castellated Gothic"; other examples are Boyington's Joliet Prison and entrance to Rosehill Cemetery. (ACC)

DRAKE HOTEL [E]. Marshall & Fox, 1920; 140 E. Walton Street (**R20**). In 1917, when Benjamin Marshall was designing a new luxury hotel for Chicago hotelier John Burroughs Drake, he selected this site with its commanding view over Lake Michigan and proximity to the affluent Gold Coast neighborhood, believing the area would soon become the city's most important and strategic location. The building's Italian Renaissance design and posh interior created an atmosphere of elegance and refinement. (MRS)

THE DRAKE HOTEL, WITH DRAKE TOWER AND PALMOLIVE BUILDING. Twelve years later, Ben Marshall designed a connecting residential building, **Drake Tower [E]** [Benjamin Marshall, 1929; 179 E. Lake Shore Drive (**R21**)], which appears here to the left of the Drake Hotel. Also visible are the Palmolive Building, adjacent to the south, and the Furniture Mart, in the distance. Marshall's prediction had proved true—in only a few years the area had grown remarkably. (GP)

BIBLIOGRAPHY

Chicago Association of Commerce and Industry. *A Guide to the City of Chicago*. (1909). Chicago: The Chicago Association of Commerce.

Condit, Carl W. *The Chicago School of Architecture: A History of Commercial and Public Building in the Chicago Area, 1875-1925*. (1964). Chicago and London: The University of Chicago Press.

Hines, Thomas S. *Burnham of Chicago: Architect and Planner*. (1974). New York: Oxford University Press.

Hitchcock, Henry-Russell. *The Architecture of H. H. Richardson and His Times*. (1961). Hamden, Connecticut: Archon Books.

Hoffmann, Donald. *The Architecture of John Wellborn Root*. (1973). Baltimore and London: Johns Hopkins University Press.

Jordy, William H. *American Buildings and Their Architects: Progressive and Academic Ideals at the Turn of the Twentieth Century*. (1976). New York: Anchor Books.

Kamin, Blair and Bob Fila. *Tribune Tower: American Landmark*. (2000). Chicago: The Tribune Company.

Knox, Janice A. and Heather Olivia Belcher. *Then & Now: Chicago's Loop*. (2002). Chicago: Arcadia Publishing.

Larson, George A. and Jay Pridmore. *Chicago Architecture and Design*. (1993). New York: Harry N. Abrams, Inc.

Lowe, David Garrard. *Lost Chicago*. (2000). New York: Watson-Guptill Publications.

Rand McNally & Company. *Souvenir Guide to Chicago*. (1912). Chicago: Rand McNally & Co.

Schulze, Franz and Kevin Harrington. *Chicago's Famous Buildings*. (1993). Chicago and London: The University of Chicago Press.

Shackleton, Robert. *The Book of Chicago*. (1920). Philadelphia: The Penn Publishing Company.

Sinkevitch, Alice (Ed.). *AIA Guide to Chicago, Second Edition*. (2004). Orlando: Harcourt, Inc.

Stamper, John W. *Chicago's North Michigan Avenue: Planning and Development, 1900–1930*. (1991). Chicago and London: The University of Chicago Press.

Steiner, Frances H. *The Architecture of Chicago's Loop*. (1998). Batavia, Illinois: Sigma Press.

Viskochil, Larry A. *Chicago at the Turn of the Century in Photographs*. (1984). New York: Dover Publications.

Wolfe, Gerard R. *Chicago: In and Around the Loop*. (2004). New York: McGraw Hill.

Zukowsky, John, ed. *Chicago Architecture, 1872-1922: birth of a metropolis*. (1987). Munich and Chicago: Prestel-Verlag and The Art Institute of Chicago.

The following websites were also important sources:

Curt Teich Postcard Archives: http://www.lcfpd.org/teich_archives
Digital Sanborn Insurance Maps: http://sanborn.umi.com
Emporis.com (formerly Skyscrapers.com): http://www.emporis.com

IMAGE SOURCES

Dates and publishers have been provided with each postcard image when available. Generally the year listed is the postmark date, but when the publication year for a postcard is known that has been used instead and is indicated as follows:

1906 = Postmark date   **1906** = Publication date.

Publishers:

A	The Acmegraph Co., Chicago
AC	American Colortype, Chicago, New York
ACB	A.C. Bosselman & Co., New York
ACC	A.C. Co. USA
ACD	A.C. Dietsche, Detroit, Mich. and Frankfort, Germany.
AH	Alfred Holzmann, Chicago & Leipzig
AHC	A. H. Co.
AMW	Albert M. Wilson Buffalo, N.Y.
BS	B. Sebastian, Publisher, Chicago
C	Cosmo M'f'g Co. Chicago
CGC	Cameo Greeting Card Co., Chicago
CLC	Chas. Levy Circulating Co., Chicago
CP	ColourPicture Publication, Boston, Mass.
CT	Curt Teich & Co., Chicago
DB	Davidson Bros' Real Photographic Series, London & New York
DP	Detroit Publishing Co.
EA	Empire Art Co., Chicago
ECK	E.C. Kropp Co., Milwaukee; C. Kropp
EP	E. Phillips
FH	Fred Harvey
FP	Franklin Post Card Co. Chicago
GB	Gerson Bros. Chicago
GP	Grogan Photo Danville, Ill.
HCL	Hugh C. Leighton Co., Portland, Me.
IW	I Will
KK	Koelling & Klappenbach, Chicago
MN	Mills Novelty Co., Chicago
MRS	Max Rigot Selling Co., Chicago
PPS	The Process Photo Studios, Chicago
PS	P. Schmidt & Co. Chicago
R	Rotograph Co., N.Y.C.
RTS	Raphael Tuck & Sons, Providence & London
SHK	S.H. Knox & Co., Chicago & Leipzig
SSK	S.S. Kresge USA
UN	Union News Company
UP	United Post Card & Novelty Co., Chicago
VOH	V.O. Hammon Publishing Co., Chicago; also Chicago & Minneapolis
WGM	W.G. MacFarlane, Toronto, Buffalo-Leipzig

INDEX